Totalitarianism

Key Concepts in Political Theory

Charles Jones and Richard Vernon, *Patriotism*

Roger Griffin, *Fascism*

Peter J. Steinberger, *Political Judgment*

Fabian Wendt, *Authority*

Eric Mack, *Libertarianism*

Elizabeth Cohen and Cyril Ghosh, *Citizenship*

Peter Lamb, *Socialism*

Benjamin Moffitt, *Populism*

Mark Stephen Jendrysik, *Utopia*

David D. Roberts, *Totalitarianism*

Totalitarianism

David D. Roberts

polity

First published in 2020 by Polity Press

Polity Press
65 Bridge Street
Cambridge CB2 1UR, UK

Polity Press
101 Station Landing
Suite 300
Medford, MA 02155, USA

ISBN-13: 978-1-5095-3239-1
ISBN-13: 978-1-5095-3240-7(pb)

A catalogue record for this book is available from the British Library.

Library of Congress Cataloging-in-Publication Data
Names: Roberts, David D., 1943- author. I Polity Press.
Title: Totalitarianism / David D. Roberts.
Other titles: Key concepts in political theory.
Description: Medford, Massachusetts : Polity, 2020. I Series: Key concepts in political theory I Includes bibliographical references and index. I Summary: "David Roberts outlines the contours and history of totalitarianism"-- Provided by publisher.
Identifiers: LCCN 2019038605 (print) I LCCN 2019038606 (ebook) I ISBN 9781509532391 (Hardback) I ISBN 9781509532407 (Paperback) I ISBN 9781509532421 (ePUB)
Subjects: LCSH: Totalitarianism. I Totalitarianism--History.
Classification: LCC JC480 .R635 2020 (print) I LCC JC480 (ebook) I DDC 321.9--dc23
LC record available at https://lccn.loc.gov/2019038605
LC ebook record available at https://lccn.loc.gov/2019038606

Typeset in 10.5 on 12 pt Sabon
by Fakenham Prepress Solutions, Fakenham, Norfolk NR21 8NL
Printed and bound in Great Britain by CPI Group (UK) Ltd, Croydon

For further information on Polity, visit our website:
politybooks.com

Contents

1
Why Should We Care about Totalitarianism?

A new political phenomenon

Coined by an Italian anti-fascist in 1923, the term "totalitarianism" quickly became part of our vocabulary, and the concept has now been central to political discussion for almost a century. However, it has long been one of the most uncertain and controversial of the key concepts in political theory. Some critics advocate abandoning it altogether. But after surveying the uses that have been made of the category, and looking again at the most prominent cases, this book will argue that totalitarianism remains essential to understanding the modern political universe. Still, the notion has often been misused or misconstrued, so we need a deeper, recast understanding of what totalitarianism might mean.

It is not hard to explain why we should care about the political phenomena most frequently labeled totalitarian, starting with three novel experiments that emerged in Europe in the wake of World War I. These were the fascist regime in Italy, the Nazi regime in Germany, and the communist regime in the Soviet Union, especially as it settled out the 1930s under Joseph Stalin. They were not only new but largely unanticipated, though in retrospect we can see foreshadowing in the "total mobilization" during World War I, including government coordination of the economy and manipulation of public opinion. For the influential Bulgarian-born Parisian intellectual Tzvetan Todorov, writing in 2000, the emergence of totalitarianism, leading to a long conflict with democracy, was nothing less than the central event of the twentieth century.[1]

The trajectories of the Soviet, German, and Italian experiments profoundly affected not only the shape of our world but also our self-understanding, our sense of what can happen. So images of those regimes still trouble us, perhaps especially because of the violence, terror, and genocidal killing they spawned. But each was also overtly antithetical to liberal procedures and values – individualism, freedom, pluralism, representative democracy, and the distinction between public and private.

We still struggle to understand what fed those three departures from what seems the political norm. Totalitarianism has offered a way of characterizing, and possibly explaining, the most troubling features of the three regimes and what differentiates them from others, especially from liberal democracies. And thus, not surprisingly, the term has come to have overwhelmingly negative connotations of violence, domination, and oppression. Moreover, those three earlier regimes all led to failure, or even disaster, outcomes that seem to suggest the deep error of the totalitarian mode of action.

However, totalitarianism was not so obviously a negative at the time. Although it had been coined as a term of abuse by opponents, the Italian fascists promptly embraced the category in the 1920s to characterize the revolution they claimed to be engineering. Moreover, the utility of the category, and the desirability of the direction it seemed to indicate, were central to discussions among those seeking political innovation, especially on the Right, prior to World War II. By the 1930s, this discussion ranged well beyond Europe to include, for example, Turkey, Argentina, and Japan. As one of the novel possibilities on the table, totalitarianism everywhere attracted some, even as it also repelled or confused others. But what did its proponents see in it?

Especially after the Stalinist turn in the Soviet Union in the early 1930s and the advent of Hitler's regime in Germany in 1933, the term "totalitarianism" was adopted by outside observers seeking to make sense of the three novel regimes, and it came significantly to shape our understanding. Above all, it seemed a way of characterizing what was new about them. To call them totalitarian was to suggest that although their hostility to liberal democracy gave them something in common with earlier authoritarian, dictatorial, and police-state governmental systems, they could not be understood in terms of those preexisting categories. Among the factors that, in combination, made these regimes unprecedented were mass mobilization, the expansion of state sovereignty, the political monopoly of a single party, and the turn to active population engineering. The state or party could intervene in anything and everything, from the educational system to the economy.

Writing in 1954, the political scientist Karl Deutsch summed up the consensus at that point:

> Totalitarianism characteristically involves the extreme mobilization of the efforts and resources of population [*sic*] under its government. "In a democracy," runs a well-known joke, "everything that is not forbidden is permitted; under an authoritarian regime, everything that is not permitted is forbidden; under totalitarianism, everything that is not forbidden is compulsory." The citizen of a totalitarian state or culture has no time and no possessions that he could truly call his own.[2]

Though with obvious hyperbole, this formulation suggests, as a rough approximation, what differentiates totalitarianism from liberal democracy, on the one hand, and authoritarianism, on the other. Of the three, liberal democracy places the greatest premium on individual freedom, including the freedom to participate in public life. Authoritarianism, more concerned to keep society under control, restricts political participation but allows freedom within a restricted framework. Totalitarianism goes a step further and denies individual freedom altogether – not, however, simply to maximize control but to mobilize the population. That is why there is no place for privacy or even free time. And thus the insistence on compulsion. But why seek such total mobilization in the first place?

The range of totalitarianism

Although the totalitarianism category emerged in response to a particular era of political experiment, the era of the two world wars in Europe, it has also been applied more widely to a variety of political regimes, movements, aspirations, and visions – and even to non-political phenomena. The spectrum of uses has raised questions about the chronological, geographical, and topical range of the phenomena that might appropriately be considered totalitarian.

Although World War II brought about the end of the Italian and German regimes, the communist experiment continued in the Soviet Union; indeed, the Soviet Union emerged a major victor from World War II, its prestige and power much enhanced. The later 1940s saw the expansion of communism to the Soviet satellite states of east central Europe, as well as, not coincidentally, the advent of the Cold War. Despite a modicum of liberalization in the Soviet bloc after Stalin's death in 1953, totalitarianism continued to be applied to the whole Soviet system until it came crashing down from 1989 to 1991.

Meanwhile, in China the communists, led by Mao Zedong,[3] took power in 1949 and, despite fits and starts, the ensuing regime followed a direction widely labeled totalitarian until Mao's death in 1976. Thereafter, his successors pulled back from what seemed the totalitarian excesses of the Mao era. But though the Chinese system became less overtly totalitarian, it entailed significant continuities from the Mao period and certainly no embrace of multiparty democracy. Meanwhile, other communist regimes emerged in, most notably, North Korea, Cuba, Cambodia, and Vietnam, all with features widely considered totalitarian. Each developed its own particular trajectory, however, and, as in China after Mao, the totalitarian thrust seemed to dissipate in some of them.

Just as totalitarianism might have seemed to be petering out in the communist world, Islamic extremism moved to center stage, first in 1979 with the revolution that created the Islamic Republic of Iran. That regime has been labeled totalitarian, and the term has also been used to characterize other Islamist movements and regimes, most notably the self-described Islamic State in Iraq and Syria (ISIS), established in 2013. Indeed, it may characterize the whole radical political ideology that some label "Islamism" to distinguish it from Islam the religion.

Moreover, some observers see a return to totalitarianism with the recent evolution of China under Xi Jinping, or even in Russia under Vladimir Putin. And if we add phenomena like the potential abuses of new technologies, to be considered under the topical range below, it is clear that, at least as a question worth raising, totalitarianism remains current.

The question of chronological range also points to the centuries before the term was applied. Some students of modern totalitarianism have found parallels and even continuities with premodern religious millenarian movements. Others have found the origins of at least the leftist brand of totalitarianism in the maelstrom of the French Revolution. Is use of the concept to characterize earlier phenomena inherently anachronistic? Reasonable observers will continue to differ, but totalitarianism has generally been considered a specifically modern phenomenon, presupposing at least indirect experience with secular liberalism and parliamentary democracy and requiring modern technologies for mobilization and indoctrination.

Precisely as modern, moreover, totalitarianism has generally been considered a specifically secular phenomenon. But that would appear to rule out earlier millenarianism, and it might seem to call into question any association of Islamic political extremism with totalitarianism. However, even those who deem such extremism totalitarian disagree over the nature of the relationship between the modern extreme and Islamic tradition. The extreme may be specifically modern and even secular, whatever the claim of a link to religious tradition.

In terms of geographical range, there have long been questions about the applicability of totalitarianism to movements or regimes beyond the Soviet Union, Italy, and Germany during the era of the two world wars. This includes several in Europe, from Spain and Portugal to Poland and Romania. Whereas most specialists do not consider Franco's Spain totalitarian, the label is routinely applied to it by journalists and the general public. But the same question comes up concerning others outside Europe, such as Imperial Japan and Kemalist Turkey. We have seen that totalitarianism was part of political discussion in both countries during the 1930s, but whether it applies to the actual practice of those regimes is much less clear.

However we draw the lines, it is undeniable that the geographical range of totalitarianism has extended across the globe. In the wake of the Russian Revolution and the foundation of the Russian-dominated Third or Communist International (Comintern) in 1919, other communist parties in Europe and beyond were founded under the Comintern umbrella. Among them was the Chinese Communist Party, launched in 1921. In adopting the communist label, they distinguished themselves from the socialist parties of the earlier Second International and committed to following the communist model under the tutelage of Russia (which became the Soviet Union in 1922). Entailing centralized discipline and control, the communist direction was arguably totalitarian precisely as the mainstream socialist direction was not.

Totalitarianism has also been used to characterize tendencies even in liberal democracies. Critics on both the Left and the Right have sometimes claimed to discern a disturbing totalitarian potential inherent in secular modernity itself. The Left points to the modern reliance on instrumental reason and the use of knowledge for power and domination. Critiques from the libertarian Right often ran parallel as they lamented the seemingly relentless expansion of the modern state, assuming ever more powers and responsibilities, arguably at the expense of individual freedom.

From either direction, that totalitarian potential might be considerably enhanced by new methods of government surveillance through social media and the internet, or of societal manipulation through genetic profiling and engineering. But is the totalitarianism category, which was, and to some extent remains, intertwined with the era of fascism and Stalinism, sufficiently flexible to illuminate such contemporary phenomena or, with all its baggage by this point, is it more likely to throw us off?

We must keep in mind, to be sure, that our key categories inevitably evolve or even "grow" with historical experience, as the trajectory of other key concepts in political theory, such as revolution, freedom, and sovereignty, make clear. Studying more recent instances might add to what we mean or understand by totalitarianism. But though the range is not delimited in some predetermined way, such concepts may get diluted, losing analytical power, as they are stretched to encompass ever more cases. So how much can the totalitarianism category grow with new experience?

Quite apart from the question of flexibility, a tendency toward careless usage, resulting from overfamiliarity, has threatened to make the category flabby. Even in scholarly discourse, totalitarianism is often used in a largely unexamined way, and in general discussion, usage sometimes veers from dilution to over-the-top sci fi fantasy.

In a television documentary on Evelyn Cameron, a pioneering English-born photographer who settled in remote eastern Montana in the late 1890s, a British photography expert refers to her "almost totalitarian feel for the image."[4] Filmmakers, especially, have sometimes been accused of seeking total control in order to manipulate the audience. But totalitarian? Such casual usage surely waters down the category unduly.

More plausible is Anna Burns's use of the category in a recent novel to characterize the tense, oppressive, tightly controlled environment on the local level during the recent sectarian struggles in Northern Ireland.[5] All aspects of life had become intensely politicized, with no escape. But though her narrator memorably conveys the sense of stifling oppressiveness, Burns too is stretching the category because there is no totalitarian intention or system but simply the atmosphere that has resulted from the sectarian struggle itself.

Masha Gessen, a highly regarded American journalist with a Soviet background, uses "totalitarianism" more conventionally to characterize a full-scale political regime in the subtitle of her recent book *The Future is History: How Totalitarianism Reclaimed Russia*. However, she invokes the category in a casual, unthinking way, seemingly because authoritarianism, autocracy, or dictatorship would not have had the same critical bite.[6] She displays little sense of why most observers have seen Putin's Russia as merely authoritarian instead. But perhaps that consensus reflects a delimited understanding of totalitarianism. And Gessen may be onto something, despite her too casual usage. We will return to the issue when considering Putin's Russia in chapter 5.

Grounds for doubt about the category

Although "totalitarianism" continues to be widely used, some observers have come to feel that it obscures more than it illuminates. By the 1970s, it was widely charged that totalitarianism had become a mere Cold War propaganda tool to discredit the Soviet Union through association with Nazi Germany. With the collapse of the Soviet bloc and the end of the Cold War, such concerns have diminished, but they have by no means disappeared altogether.

In any case, the Cold War objection points to a more general question concerning the legitimacy of lumping fascism and communism as instances of totalitarianism when they seem so radically different, even diametrically opposed, in origin, ideology, and initial purpose. Moreover, the communists eliminated most forms of private property while the fascists did not. Both fascist regimes, though especially the Italian, rested on compromise with preexisting elites and institutions. The Soviets did away with the old regime far more systematically. Even if totalitarianism might account for certain common features, lumping fascist and communist regimes under the one category might seem inherently to be glossing over too much.

In their important co-edited volume, provocatively entitled *Beyond Totalitarianism: Stalinism and Nazism Compared*, Michael Geyer and Sheila Fitzpatrick do not object to the category on the grounds of its political valences. Rather, they worry that, as applied to the Nazi and Soviet cases, it has led to an overemphasis on commonalities at the expense of deeper differences, as indicated, they argue, by the innovative new research, conducted without the prism of totalitarianism, conveyed in their volume.[7] In a similar vein, Michael David-Fox, introducing a book treating Soviet Russia and Nazi Germany as entangled histories, writes that since 1997 "many scholars have begun to search for new ways of looking at the two fields that challenge or go beyond the older comparisons written in the vein of totalitarianism theory."[8] Like Geyer and Fitzpatrick, he takes it for granted that, even if it might have been useful earlier, the totalitarianism approach must be left behind if we are to develop fresh insights.

Use of the totalitarianism category surely did reflect Cold War hostility to the Soviet Union on occasion, but resistance to the category on the part of those relatively sympathetic to the Soviet experiment also reflected Cold War pressures. In any case, the possibility of misuse does not in itself undermine the utility of the category, either as an analytical and comparative tool or as a way of characterizing aspirations and dynamics in practice. Put differently, the fact that it could serve Cold War purposes does not mean that this was the primary purpose, or that it did so in every case.

But I noted that doubts about lumping together fascism and communism cut deeper. Few would deny that *some* combination of similarities and differences was at work, but those objecting to lumping may not do justice to the real-world dynamic bringing the particular fascist and communist regimes at issue closer together than an abstract consideration might recognize.

The difference in originating aspirations does not rule out such commonalities, especially in light of the Leninist break from orthodox Marxism and the Stalinist break from within Leninism. Once the Soviets began pursuing "socialism in one country," their Marxist underpinnings, which might seem especially to differentiate them from fascism, became ever more tenuous, even mythical. It remains the case that the Soviets made an anti-capitalist revolution as the fascists did not, but the Soviets and fascists were moving in a common statist, or arguably totalitarian, direction as an alternative to free market capitalism.

The fascists had concluded that the problem was not capitalism or private property but the wider liberal culture, which seemed responsible for what was most objectionable about capitalism. A change in political culture might yield a qualitatively superior relationship between the political and economic spheres even if major aspects of private property remained. For their part, the Soviets concluded that socialism in one country required crash industrialization based on forced collectivization in agriculture – a process very much directed from the top. Whether the break came with Lenin or with Stalin, the actual Soviet regime ended up sufficiently overlapping with the fascist regimes that not only can it be compared with them but it can fruitfully be considered together with them as instances of totalitarianism. It must be emphasized, however, that though totalitarianism cuts across the conventional Left–Right axis, it does not replace that axis, which remains essential for certain questions.

At the same time, we must ask how much difference the persistence of preexisting elites and institutions actually made. They could be co-opted, even caught up in synergistic relationships with genuine fascists, so that it may be misleading to assume that one side had to be winning and the other losing and that conservative elites were marginalizing genuine fascists. Even in this particular, it may be too easy to overplay differences between the fascist and the Soviet regimes.

A second objection concerns the image that had come to surround totalitarianism, based on a "structural model" positing top-down "total domination" as the aim, whether to serve power for its own sake or to pursue some fanatical ideological vision. Though it may linger in our imaginations, that model came to be largely rejected by specialists as research showed how chaotic, messy, and ultimately out of control the putatively totalitarian regimes actually were. Thus some came to find totalitarianism singularly inappropriate, even for dealing with Hitler's Germany and Stalin's Russia. In his widely admired study of the two regimes, published in 2004, Richard Overy found totalitarianism almost a joke, a "political-science fantasy" presupposing "domination through fear by psychopathic tyrants" who wield "total, unlimited power."[9] To discuss these regimes in terms of totalitarianism seems bound to throw us off.

The brief defense against this objection is to ask who says it was all about total control in the first place? And even insofar as, for whatever reason, that was part of the aim, totalitarianism might plausibly be understood as an aspiration, a tendency, with no implication of complete realization. Could we recast the category as a novel mode of collective action that proved, in practice, to entail a particular tendency to spin out of control?

A third objection concerns the use of totalitarianism as a differentiating principle, especially to distinguish genuinely fascist regimes from other instances of right-wing, authoritarian dictatorship, such as Franco's Spain or Salazar's Portugal. Many recent authorities take its use for this purpose for granted, whether explicitly or implicitly. But scholars concerned primarily with cases other than Germany and Italy have charged that the totalitarian–authoritarian dichotomy tends to overstate differences, making the real-world distinctions too neat. Moreover, it obscures the interactive relationship between the fascist regimes and those that, though not fully fascist, were eager to learn from the seeming successes of the fascist regimes. And thus they cannot be understood as merely conservative, traditionalist, or authoritarian. The problem is that totalitarianism seems to imply an either–or approach that obscures the dynamic relationships of the time and thus fails to account for the novelty of these movements and regimes.

But even if the totalitarian–authoritarian dichotomy was long overdone, totalitarianism, appropriately nuanced, can still serve as a differentiating category. This entails simply loosening the dichotomy, making it less either–or. It remains the case that if any political formation was not seeking or moving in a totalitarian direction, it was not fascism.

In short, though these objections force us to nuance our thinking, they do not indicate that totalitarianism has outlived its usefulness – or was misguided in the first place. However, the category has been left in a somewhat anomalous situation overall. Whereas some see it as outmoded, others still use it but sometimes unthinkingly. As presently applied, in scholarly discussion and more widely, it can indeed become formulaic, compromising understanding, so reaction against it has been healthy up to a point. But some eschew it for reasons that seem merely tendentious or short-sighted. If we keep a more open mind, we might see how a recast notion of totalitarianism can better interpret new researches like those organized by Geyer and Fitzpatrick and David-Fox, deepen our understanding of the three earlier regimes, and illuminate more recent phenomena as well.

In any case, we must think of totalitarianism simply as an aspiration and direction, not as some system that could ever be completely realized. If it is to be appropriately flexible, moreover, totalitarianism cannot be confined by a formal definition or checklist. But we already have a working conception, including statist intervention and total mobilization, and we will find additional characteristics indicating a novel mode of collective action, emerging early in chapter 3.

The scope for learning from experience

For decades, the failures of the earlier totalitarian experiments bred confidence in the superiority of liberal democracy and a concomitant assumption that totalitarianism could never recur from within the western mainstream. But in the volatile world of the twenty-first century, we are less prone to such complacent liberal triumphalism. There are obviously those today who reject the whole panoply of liberal values and procedures and, on that basis, support movements or regimes we find troubling. Insofar as we seek to prevent any recurrence of totalitarianism in the West, surely we can learn by better engaging the earlier phenomena labeled totalitarian. The question is how we do so most fruitfully. What understanding of totalitarianism might better serve that aim?

Writing in 1967, the noted American intellectual Irving Howe asserted that none of the theorists of totalitarianism could tell us the "ultimate purpose" of the Nazis or Stalinists. Howe doubted that such questions could presently be answered and suggested that perhaps they were not even genuine problems: "A movement in which terror and irrationality play so great a role may finally have no goal beyond terror and irrationality; to search for an ultimate end that can be significantly related to its immediate activity may itself be a rationalist fallacy."[10] We assume that there had to have been a reason, in other words, and we may be tempted to make one up.

It is useful to be reminded of this possible fallacy, but Howe, in relying so heavily on terror and irrationality, was falling into essentialism and teleological thinking, enduring pitfalls that we will consider in the ensuing chapters. Thus he was too quick to give up on the possibility of historical understanding. The way out is simply to engage our subjects more deeply and to probe more deeply into the history that connects them with us. From within such a framework, we can better understand origins, assess responsibility, honor the victims, and serve the worthy aim of "never again."

2
The Career of a Concept

We already have a sense that the concept of totalitarianism emerged in a specific context; it was not just "there," ready to be applied, enabling us to determine whether this or that was totalitarian or not. And we need a sense of the history of the concept itself to understand both how it has come down to us and what it has meant along the way. By now, a dominant conception is taken for granted by authoritative recent observers from Federico Finchelstein to Peter Baehr to Richard Shorten, with variations evident in the wider culture. But this dominant notion sometimes impedes understanding, even questioning and imagination, especially because of certain pitfalls, most basically reductionism, theological thinking, essentialism, and moralism. Pinpointing those pitfalls as we trace the career of the concept, showing how they throw us off, will help us see how to recast totalitarianism.

As understood by insiders at the time

We first need some sense of what the category meant to those caught up in the novel political experiments prior to World War II, before its connotations became so profoundly negative. The Soviets largely ignored the category, but it was prominent, though controversial, among fascists and those interested in fascism on the Right. Among its leading Italian proponents was Giovanni Gentile, who was already a noted philosopher before joining forces with fascism in 1923, and who was soon trumpeting totalitarianism as the key to fascist self-understanding. Gentile's thinking is hard to pin down and indeed is easily caricatured. But the Soviet specialist Abbott Gleason, in his valuable survey of the uses of the term "totalitarianism," found Gentile's conception of the totalitarian state "extraordinary" and "prophetic" and concluded that "Gentile deserves to be called the first philosopher of totalitarianism."[1] However, even Gleason was too quick to conflate Gentile's thinking with "conservative Hegelianism," on the one hand, and "George Orwell's demonic visions," on the other.[2]

Gentile had some regard for Marx, but he concluded that what the modern secular world required was not a socioeconomic revolution against capitalism but a cultural-political revolution with two mutually reinforcing dimensions. On the one hand, it was more comprehensively to encompass the educational system to marshal and focus the human ethical capacity, so that everyone would come to share in the sense of total ongoing responsibility for the future. On the other hand, the reach of the state was to be expanded to begin shaping the world more coherently and systematically. In inviting, even demanding, more constant and direct participation, expanded collective action would itself marshal and focus the human ethical capacity.[3]

Gentile specified a new mode of collective action through what he termed explicitly a totalitarian ethical state, a notion that surely seems oxymoronic on first encounter. Put simply, as our sense of responsibility grows, we need to expand our capacity to act, to shape what the world becomes. In concentrating and extending power through the state, we enhance our collective freedom to act. Indeed, freedom requires that the state's reach be potentially limitless, totalitarian. So to make the state totalitarian does not limit our freedom, as would seem the case from a liberal perspective, but enables us to exercise it more extensively, effectively, and responsibly.

In that sense, the totalitarian state does not stand opposed to the freedom of differentiated individuals, as we tend to assume it must. On the contrary, it values individuation and presupposes anything but a lifeless uniformity. Each individual is a precious fount of human ethical capacity, and that capacity must be nurtured and respected within the totalitarian ethical state. Still, though our commitments will differ, we are to live lives of total public commitment, total responsibility. All are to be involved, all the time. There is no place for contemplative withdrawal, or self-cultivation, or mere alienation. We will note the place of Gentile's vision in the practice of fascist Italy in the next chapter.

It is striking that the German Nazis invoked Gentile during the mid-1930s as they judged totalitarianism inappropriate for their own regime, even as they found it applicable to Fascist Italy. At issue, first, was the extent to which an emphasis on the state, even a new *totalitarian* state, inherently meant a premium on fixed procedures and codified law – on writing it all down. At issue, second, was the extent to which any such premium was incongruent with the form of collective action necessary in what seemed a newly unpredictable, open-ended world. Even within each regime such questions occasioned tension and debate. Whereas Camillo Pellizzi, stressing provisionality and openness, portrayed laws as mere hieroglyphs in the sand, Mussolini's minister of justice Alfredo Rocco accented codification and the predictability of law even as the state's reach expanded indefinitely.

Rocco's legal rationalism, especially, stood diametrically opposed to the Nazi conception of law based on race, blood, the *Volk* (people), and the will of the Führer. Their sense of the requirements for the necessary action led the Nazis to resist any premium on codification of the law, no matter how wide and even total its scope. Action required flexibility, including the scope for improvised response. In that sense, Nazism did move more radically beyond traditional state ideas, but that is no warrant for concluding, in simple dualistic terms, that Nazism was totalitarian while Italian fascism was merely traditionalist or authoritarian. To codify the law was indeed less "dynamic" in the sense that the Nazis had in mind, but to expand to totality the scope for codified law might be seen as equally totalitarian. The key is the total reach, not the mode of dynamism envisioned.

A major German participant in this discussion was Carl Schmitt, a leading jurist in Germany even before Hitler came to power in 1933. Although his take on the issues departed from the Nazi mainstream, soon leaving him isolated within the Nazi regime, he has attracted considerable attention in recent decades.

Schmitt welcomed the advent of Nazism as an antidote to what seemed the chaotic, excessively pluralistic expansion of the German state in response to growing societal demands under the Weimar Republic. In this light, the top-down coordination – *Gleichschaltung* – that marked the first stage of the Nazi revolution could be understood as a welcome restoration of state sovereignty and authority. But as a response to the Weimar crisis and all it had revealed about modern politics, the Nazi revolution had to be more innovative than that. In his *Staat, Bewegung, Volk* (State, Movement, People) of 1933, Schmitt offered what he portrayed as a new synthesis, pointing beyond the liberal dualism of state and society, to show how the state could encompass the expanded societal content. In doing so, he thought he was doing justice to the novelty – and primacy – of Nazism at the same time. The state was no longer a sphere of fixed law that determines the political element but was now determined by it – by the movement and its leadership.[4]

But Schmitt proved symptomatically ambiguous in treating the interface of restoration and novelty, of static and dynamic, of society, politics, and state. To a considerable extent, he was still featuring the state's conventional role of maintaining order by adjudicating conflicts and harmonizing contending social forces. At the Nazi party congress of September 1934, his conservative notion that the people was to be ruled aroused protest and was rejected. From the Nazi perspective, the people, spearheaded by the movement, was the agent.[5] Though he had departed from the conservative traditionalists up to a point, Schmitt's thinking remained too conventional and static to grasp why the Nazis insisted that the "movement" as opposed to a new state, was the vehicle for the essential modern dynamism.

By implication, the point for the Nazis was not merely to impose order on a newly more demanding society, though, in light of the chaotic tendencies of Weimar, a new discipline did seem necessary. Such discipline, however, served the deeper aim of making society – the people – into a dynamic instrument for ongoing action. In comparison, Schmitt's conception remained "pre-totalitarian": individual moral response fuels sociopolitical antagonism, and politics simply harmonizes the conflicting forces, as opposed to mobilizing, nurturing, and channeling societal energies for dynamic collective ends. Thus the Nazi charge that Schmitt was a neo-Hegelian positing the primacy of the state vis-à-vis the *Volk*.

Beyond Italy and Germany, those seeking systematic alternatives to liberal democracy or conservative authoritarianism sometimes claimed to embrace totalitarianism, though its meaning to them was often fuzzy, subject to wishful thinking. To some extent, in fact, totalitarianism was merely a fashionable slogan or myth.

Before winning the Spanish Civil War, the insurgent Nationalist leader General Francisco Franco observed in a 1938 interview that his new state would be structured like the totalitarian regimes, such as those in Italy and Germany, but with specifically Spanish characteristics. By 1944, many adherents of the Franco regime perceived it as totalitarian but not always with approval. Some called for an end to totalitarianism and the reestablishment of a traditionalist Catholic monarchy. Even those favoring anti-democratic authoritarian dictatorship might take totalitarianism as a negative.

All over Europe and beyond, some found totalitarianism more appropriate than fascism to characterize their own innovations, yet the relationship between the two categories was never clear. In Greece, proponents of the new regime of General Ioannis Metaxas during the later 1930s avoided using "fascist," opting instead for the more ambiguous "totalitarian." Metaxas himself was explicit, however, that totalitarianism meant precisely that his regime, as innovative, had something in common not only with the two fascist regimes but also with the Soviet regime as post-democratic.[6]

As a critical and analytical concept

Especially after the Stalinist turn in the Soviet Union by 1930 and the advent of the Nazi regime in Germany in 1933, totalitarianism came to be used by critical outsiders trying to get a handle on the new political phenomena. To be sure, some continued to view the conventional Left–Right axis as fundamental, but others sensed that these experiments could be, had to be, treated together as something new, unanticipated, transcending the Left–Right divide. Thus the appeal of the totalitarianism category. And with fascism and Soviet totalitarianism seemingly live options, adversaries took the overall totalitarian challenge seriously indeed. An array of figures could be considered, but let us focus on two, Peter Drucker and James Burnham, each of whom hoped that democracy could be preserved even as the outcome seemed anything but certain on the eve of World War II.

Born in Austria, Drucker found his way to the United States, where he eventually became a well-known management consultant. In 1939, he published *The End of Economic Man: The Origins of Totalitarianism*, a book of great passion, much airy speculation, yet also undoubted insights – insights that tended to get lost once the fascist regimes had been swept away.

As Drucker saw it, "economic man" came to an end with the failure of liberal capitalist society to achieve through the economic sphere the freedom and equality that, thanks to Christianity, had come to seem essential to the western world. That failure opened the way for the totalitarian experiments of both fascism and communism. To be sure, as Drucker was quick to point out, Soviet communism in its early years had been based precisely on the economic conception of society. But with all the anomalies resulting from its crash industrialization drive, belief in the attainability of freedom and equality through Marxist socialism collapsed, and the Soviet Union became fundamentally similar to Germany and Italy by the end the 1930s. They were comparably totalitarian.[7]

For Drucker, then, totalitarianism was the alternative when neither capitalism nor socialism could deliver on the promise of freedom and equality. But it entailed not simply manipulation from above. Rather, he posited a more reciprocal relationship between leaders and led; the leaders were genuinely seeking to address the crisis.

And this meant that "the most fundamental, though least publicized, feature of totalitarianism in Italy and Germany is the attempt to substitute noneconomic for economic satisfactions, rewards, and considerations as the basis for the rank, function, and position of the individual in industrial society."[8] This was fascism's social miracle, making it possible to preserve the necessarily unequal industrial system of production. It required the new organizations for youth, for women, and for leisure time that have long been associated with totalitarianism. For Drucker, the leisure organizations were the centerpiece, providing noneconomic benefits such as concerts and vacations, and promoting a measure of social equality to compensate for continued economic inequality. But as a poor substitute for real equality, this social equality could only ease the problem, not overcome it.[9]

Drucker astutely noted that totalitarian organization, seemingly indicating superiority over the liberal mainstream, becomes its own justification. But though effective up to a point, such organization proved to entail the inefficiency of countless conflicting authorities, a hollowing to nothing but a putatively infallible leader, and a tendency to spin out of control.[10] The bottom line was that totalitarianism was not a viable solution to the crisis, but by implication it could be a recurring temptation until a more viable solution was found.

Shortly after Drucker's book appeared, the American political theorist James Burnham published a still more influential study, *The Managerial Revolution: What is Happening in the World*, in 1941. Unlike Drucker, Burnham was not concerned with some putative spiritual crisis but with the relentless modern drive for economic efficiency. It had displaced free market capitalism with "managerialism," involving the structuring of large corporations as well as economic coordination and planning. For Burnham, that managerial revolution was central to modernity, and in light of its essential characteristics it easily could point toward totalitarianism.

Nonetheless, Burnham concluded that certain features of managerialism favored the democratic outcome he preferred. For example, in totalitarian systems, including the Soviet Union, it was hard to get the accurate readings of public attitudes that centralized planning required. But Burnham cautioned against over-optimism because other aspects of the managerial revolution tended to undercut some essential aspects of democracy, such as independent economic foundations for opposition political groups. So managerialism bred a tendency toward the monopoly of a single party.[11]

Along the way, Burnham offered some astute observations on the Soviet, German, and Italian regimes, all of which he found overtly totalitarian in seeking to coordinate nearly every aspect of life. And the enterprise could only have been modern, he insisted, because it presupposed the modern technology, especially in communications and transportation, necessary to coordinate so much so intimately.[12]

The quest for deep historical roots

At about the same time as Drucker and Burnham, a number of scholars began seeking intellectual antecedents for the troubling recent political phenomena. The Austrian-born Karl Popper (1902–94), on his way to becoming one of the century's most influential philosophers of science, published *The Open Society and Its Enemies* in two volumes in 1945, though he wrote it between 1938 and 1943. In the introduction to a subsequent edition, he contended that what we now call totalitarianism belongs to a tradition as old as our civilization itself.[13] And in the first volume Popper famously, or notoriously, traced it back to Greek philosophy and especially to Plato, though what he called "the high tide of prophecy" was reached only in the nineteenth century with Hegel and Marx, covered in the second volume.[14] In treating intellectual antecedents, he was not positing influence but seeking to account for a recurring orientation or mode of thought.

Popper labeled the enemy "historicism," using a problematic term in a somewhat idiosyncratic way as a quest for predictive laws of historical development. Finding it hard to make sense of change, the Greeks had sought the higher, stable laws that they assumed must govern change; without them, the world appeared capricious and chaotic. In recent times, the same basic mentality had led some to feature a chosen race or class, each on the basis of a putative law of human development. More generally, variations on historicism emerge as a response to periods of revolutionary upheaval, which induce a dizzying sense that nothing is stable.[15] Among other things, historicism stood opposed to the critical and rational methods of science, which warranted piecemeal, as opposed to utopian, modes of social engineering.[16]

Though Hegel and Marx remain prominent in discussions of intellectual antecedents, Popper's way of implicating Plato and the Greeks has few defenders. Certainly Plato, concerned with the requirements for good order in society, favored something like an autocracy of the wise, but the mode of control he envisioned did not approximate modern totalitarianism.[17] Moreover, Popper's thinking in *The Open Society* has come to seem too dichotomous, ahistorical, and teleological. He allows for essentially two orientations, open and closed. The turn to a closed society is most likely in times of upheaval, but the tendency is ahistorical. We know what totalitarianism was – the closed society – and asking who would favor that, and why, can only yield a delimited range of answers, essentially an intolerance for ambiguity leading to a kind of utopianism. The whole schema has come to seem too limiting.

In *The Origins of Totalitarian Democracy*, first published in 1952, the Polish-born Israeli scholar Jacob Talmon found the sources of totalitarianism considerably closer to the present than Popper, but still not as close as Burnham. For Talmon, totalitarian dictatorship was a child of the Enlightenment, the darker side of the modern democratic age. The two currents emerged side by side in the eighteenth century. Central to the totalitarian side were Jean-Jacques Rousseau and the Jacobins, who gave rise to a radical tradition that carried on into the twentieth century. Tensions between the totalitarian and the liberal democratic currents have continued ever since; Talmon found this conflict the most important issue of his time.[18]

However, he also recognized a different bifurcation, of Left and Right, within totalitarianism itself. The Right was concerned with a collective entity, whether state, nation, or race, while the Left was concerned with individuals. Moreover, the Left posited universal human values based on reason, values denied by the Right. And whereas the Left believed humanity to be perfectible, the Right found humanity weak and corrupt. In seeking the origins of totalitarian democracy, Talmon was concerned only with the Left.[19]

And for his purposes it was the contrast between totalitarian democracy and liberal democracy that most mattered. The former combined political messianism, positing a preordained harmonious scheme of things, and an extreme version of eighteenth-century rationalism, which suggested that uniformly rational behavior could be expected in a properly integrated society.[20] But totalitarians had trouble reconciling this state with freedom for existing individuals. Genuine liberty, they assumed, must coincide with virtue and reason, so people need to be considered not as they are but as they are meant to be. Insofar as they are *not* as they are meant to be – free and virtuous – they can be ignored or coerced. Under proper conditions, there would be no conflict between spontaneity and duty, or between freedom and virtue, so the need for coercion would disappear.

When, in the real world, liberty and virtue proved to conflict on occasion, liberal democracy shrank from coercion, recognizing political systems as pragmatic contrivances and settling for trial and error. But the totalitarian strand continued. Whereas for totalitarianism the political is all encompassing, liberal democracy posits spheres of personal and even collective endeavor outside politics.[21]

Though from a very different angle, Talmon's diagnosis converged with Popper's in suggesting that totalitarians were unable to deal with historical openness, change, and uncertainty. Both Popper and Talmon insisted that we must accept the inevitability of conflict and proceed by trial and error. And Talmon, like Popper, implied that the underlying source of totalitarianism was an enduring psychological propensity that came to the fore especially with the familiar disruptions of the modern period. Talmon was contemptuous of this orientation: "human life can never reach a state of repose. That imagined repose is another name for the security offered by a prison, and the longing for it may in a sense be an expression of cowardice and laziness, of the inability to face the fact that life is a perpetual and never resolved crisis."[22]

Here we find a prime example of reductionist deflating, making the totalitarian democratic impulse a pathological psychological tendency to be cured. From this angle, a historically specific layer was certainly involved in the emergence of totalitarianism, but the key to understanding is the incapacity of some people, in light of ahistorical psychological propensities, to handle the healthy liberal pluralism and openness that also became possible with the modern world.

We noted that Talmon found parallels between totalitarian democracy and earlier millenarian movements. The most influential effort to draw out such parallels was Norman Cohn's in concluding the 1961 edition of *The Pursuit of the Millennium*. There he explicitly asserted not only parallels but literal continuity between earlier Christian millenarianism and modern totalitarianism.[23]

To say that earlier messianic movements inspired later totalitarians is not to say that they were themselves instances of totalitarianism, but Cohn came close to doing so. Such earlier millenarianism, he contended, yielded "a group of a peculiar kind, a true prototype of a modern totalitarian party: a restlessly dynamic and utterly ruthless group which, obsessed by the apocalyptic phantasy and filled with the conviction of its own infallibility, set itself infinitely above the rest of humanity and recognized no claims save that of its own supposed mission."[24]

Obviously, Cohn did not share Burnham's emphasis on the defining role of modern technology in totalitarianism. As Cohn saw it, what set the Soviet and the Nazi experiments apart, especially in their early years, was precisely their millenarianism, endowing conflicts with transcendent significance. Both were inspired by archaic fantasies, by earlier popular apocalyptic lore. Each saw itself as the protagonist in a final eschatological drama, in which the chosen people would destroy the agents of corruption – whether the Jews or the wealthy bourgeoisie – thereby renewing the world and ending history. Moreover, Cohn explicitly accounted Marx a millenarian, so the eruption of millenarianism in Bolshevik Russia was not merely a Russian atavism.[25]

But why did such millenarianism became more powerful in the twentieth century than it was in the Middle Ages? In both periods, Cohn maintained, millenarianism offered promise to "rootless and desperate" people in "a society where traditional norms and relationships are disintegrating."[26]

It appealed to surplus populations, people on the margins lacking the material and emotional support provided by traditional social groups.[27]

Cohn continues to have some resonance, but most have found his account overstated. Richard Shorten, writing in 2012, criticized what he called Cohn's improbably strong claim about historical derivation and continuity.[28] Earlier, Talmon, too, had pinpointed a vital difference, even as he noted parallels between earlier messianic movements and certain modern movements. The earlier, as religious, entailed sporadic outbursts aiming to break away from society. The latter, as political, was concerned with governing society as a whole – and, by implication, was more genuinely totalitarian.[29]

Although there remains plausible disagreement over the degree to which utopianism lies at the root of modern totalitarianism, Cohn arguably overstated totalitarianism's messianic element. Moreover, in repairing to rootlessness and desperation, he, too, embraced a reductionist strategy, one that was common when he was writing but that raises at least yellow flags today. It might characterize the specifically millenarian segment, but it is too limited to account for modern totalitarianism overall.

George Orwell's dystopia

Meanwhile, George Orwell (born Eric Blair) published his famed dystopian novel *Nineteen Eighty-Four* in 1949. Already well known as an innovative essayist and partisan of progressive causes, Orwell had published *Animal Farm* to considerable acclaim in 1946. It was a transparent allegory, pillorying the anti-egalitarian outcome of Soviet communism to that point, an outcome that seemed radically to belie the rhetoric of the Soviet regime. The scenario in *Nineteen Eighty-Four* was even more obviously patterned on Stalin's Soviet Union, but Orwell had Nazi Germany in mind as well. The novel has long been taken as a treatment of totalitarianism in general, not just Stalinism or even communism.

In writing the book, Orwell was engaged in a two-pronged effort to promote a democratic form of socialism. First, with the Soviet Union being maligned in Britain and elsewhere early in the Cold War, Soviet sympathizers came to its defense. But for Orwell they were too quick to turn a blind eye to Soviet totalitarian abuses. With *Nineteen Eighty-Four*, Orwell wanted to confront the public with this negative side and thereby to build support for an alternative, democratic form of socialism. Second, he wanted to undercut James Burnham's implication in *The Managerial Revolution* that Soviet communism was one plausible, possibly viable, way the managerial revolution might go.[30]

Some of Orwell's portrayal is by now so familiar as to approach cliché. Big Brother, clearly patterned on Stalin, is the focal point of a system dominated by the party, though he does not appear in the novel and may not really exist. In any case, "Big Brother is watching you" – and possibly those in charge literally watched everybody all the time, through two-way TV screens. Universal surveillance and thought police to root out "thoughtcrime" were essential to the system. People who were considered suspicious simply disappeared, always during the night, their one-time existence denied and then forgotten.

The positive, such as it is, is cemented by a radical, though still only gradual reform of language to produce "Newspeak," eliminating words to narrow the range of thought, so that "thoughtcrime" becomes impossible. But though Newspeak is radically simplifying, it encompasses the complexity of "doublethink," a strategy to overcome our own memory, even to think contradictory thoughts simultaneously while forgetting that we are doing so. Doublethink was especially characteristic of, and important to, the leaders, making fanaticism and cynicism possible at the same time.[31]

In an essay written in 1946, Orwell observed that organized lying is integral to totalitarianism, not, as is sometimes claimed, a temporary expedient. The totalitarian ruling caste must be thought infallible, and thus must invent history to cover over mistakes: "Totalitarianism demands, in fact, the continuous alteration of the past, and in the long run probably demands a disbelief in the very existence of objective truth."[32]

The noted novelist Thomas Pynchon found in *Nineteen Eighty-Four* "as dark an ending as can be imagined" because those in power prove able to get inside the heads of the major protagonists, Winston and Julia, in a way that Julia had thought impossible. Insisting that feelings are impregnable, she had clung to the difference between mere confession and genuine, inner betrayal.[33] But Winston and Julia are indeed led to betray each other. Moreover, we can be made to believe anything, even, if it should be held necessary, that $2 + 2 = 5$, insofar as the system can exploit the particular traumas of each us in "Room 101." By the end, Winston is entirely broken: "everything was all right, the struggle was finished. He had won the victory over himself. He loved Big Brother."[34]

But what is driving the system, what is the motivation, the purpose? We find no critique of totalist ideology or residual Marxism in the novel; it is not a matter of ideological fanaticism but something more cynical and sinister. The underlying purpose, according to O'Brien, the most authoritative spokesman we hear, is simply to maintain power, entirely for its own sake. Thus the need for continuous war, not victory; the purpose of war was to keep the structure of society intact.[35]

But reduction to the banal power drive, total control, constant surveillance, and fear tells us next to nothing about the origins, purposes, or even actual functioning of the Soviet or any totalitarian regime. None of the three classic regimes evolved in anything like Orwell's way. He entirely missed the totalitarian tendency to spin out of control or to bog down, even to peter out. However, misleading though it is, *Nineteen Eighty-Four* helped fix a stereotypical image of what totalitarianism portends. Writing in 1967, Irving Howe concluded that Orwell has "given us the most graphic vision of totalitarianism that has yet been composed."[36]

The ongoing influence of Hannah Arendt

Hannah Arendt's *The Origins of Totalitarianism* first appeared in 1951, a bit before Talmon's *The Origins of Totalitarian Democracy*, but Arendt published an augmented second edition in 1958, and it is in that form that the book has remained known.[37] It is certainly the most influential book on totalitarianism ever written, achieving something like canonical status. Arendt was a charismatic Jewish-German woman, trained in philosophy. Forced to flee Europe in 1941, she found her way to the United States. Although her book was by no means a personal account, her passion, her determination to get to the bottom of Nazism and totalitarianism, made it seductively dramatic.

Like Popper and Talmon, Arendt was concerned with deep origins, but her focus was very different, as she sought to back up to the conditions of possibility for the totalitarian departures of the twentieth century. For her, this was not remotely a matter of intellectual antecedents, as it was for Popper and to a lesser extent also for Talmon; nor was it a matter of sources of inspiration, as for Cohn a bit later. At the same time, however, Arendt found something deeper than the immediate crises of World War I, political instability, and the Depression to have been at work. Although in a very different way than for Talmon, the most basic categories of the political tradition in the West since the Enlightenment were in question.

Arendt saw totalitarianism as a unique, unprecedented macro-event that could only be understood through a deeply historical approach. To grasp the genesis of something so radically new, she found it essential to avoid social science definition and classification, which, as she saw it, tended to seek explanation in terms of something prior, already known. This necessarily deflected from what was most new and troubling.[38] Still, controversy quickly surrounded her book; critics found it speculative and called for a more circumspect empirical approach.

In a sense, Arendt came at the problem of totalitarianism from two directions. On the one hand, she sought to identify long-term socioeconomic, political, and cultural changes that had altered the framework, making it possible for totalitarians to attempt what they did. On the other hand, she asked what had motivated that attempt.

To get at the former, Arendt sought to delineate what had happened between the Enlightenment and the advent of the totalitarian regimes. It had nothing to do with Talmon's syndrome, entailing a totalitarian direction emerging full-blown from the Enlightenment. As Arendt saw it, the totalitarian possibility had taken over a century to crystalize, and it required considerable experience with modern democratic politics. In contrast with Popper and Talmon, moreover, she implicitly recognized that serious problems with parliamentary democracy had surfaced as it emerged in practice, so criticism was plausible, as was the quest for a radical alternative.

Arendt was pinpointing elements that any convincing account of the origins of totalitarianism must encompass: the place of interests and rights, the scope for political virtue, the changing relationship between the economic and political spheres, the generation and expansion of power, and the new sense of history that she had in mind in accenting "motion" and dynamism.[39] But how did it all come together, and how did it interface with totalitarian aspirations?

During the course of the nineteenth century, as Arendt saw it, the nation-state evolved in a particular way because of a combination of particularism – the pursuit of narrow economic interests – and imperialism. An earlier premium on civic virtue, one of the legacies of the Enlightenment, was marginalized as the state disintegrated into the arena of the clash of particular socioeconomic interests – a clash only superficially masked as party politics. Just as the degeneration into societal particularism compromised the state as a stable sphere of law, expansion beyond the nation-state required encompassing groups that were outside the sphere of citizenship, rights, and legal protections. The weakening of both stable law and human rights opened the way for the totalitarians subsequently to operate unchecked, to seek and even to begin exercising total power.

Meanwhile, traditional classes were breaking down, leaving society an undifferentiated mass – mass society. In a society of masses as opposed to classes, one could hope to mobilize and manipulate people as isolated individuals, as automatons. But why would anyone seek to do so? It was not necessary for capitalist profit, and Arendt insisted explicitly that the point was not simply power for its own sake.

She portrayed total domination as a means to implement and confirm a prior ideology – Marxism in the case of the Soviet Union, social Darwinism in the case of Nazi

Germany.[40] The common embrace of a totalist, deterministic ideology was central to the convergence of the Nazi and Stalinist regimes, but Arendt noted an important difference: To create totalitarian rule, "Stalin had first to create artificially that atomized society which had been prepared for the Nazis in Germany by historical circumstances."[41]

In any case, as Arendt saw it, each of the ideologies was unrealistic, especially because the claim of total explanation was incompatible with human freedom and creativity, which make history unpredictable. Because of that incongruity, the totalitarians had to force reality to fit their essentially fictitious ideologies. Totalitarian practice, with all its aggressiveness, took place "only for ideological reasons: to make the world consistent, to prove that its respective supersense has been right."[42] So the totalitarians had concluded, if only implicitly, that they could not simply sit back and let history or nature take its course – or simply apply the ideology as if a blueprint. In Arendt's own terms, those ideologies were important but not remotely sufficient to specify the modes of action adopted.

Arendt famously claimed that the Nazi and Soviet concentration and forced labor camps revealed the underlying dynamic of totalitarianism. In the otherworldly setting of these camps, the totalitarians managed to reduce creative human beings to predictable automatons, marionettes, merely conditioned reflexes, and thereby to create the predictable world their ideologies envisioned. Only in such a setting, where the free human personality could be readily manipulated, could the totalitarians actually achieve the total domination they sought.[43]

Outside the camps, the totalitarians could approximate that control and predictability by keeping people in motion. Such perpetual motion, or dynamism, required terror to atomize society and thereby enable the rulers to do the work of history or nature, without interference from human spontaneity, freedom, and creativity. But such dynamism was ultimately self-destructive.[44]

Peter Baehr contends that Arendt, in taking the camps as archetypal, best captured the nightmare, surreal quality of totalitarianism and its rupture from normal standards – even normal crimes.[45] But Arendt attracted some astute critics almost immediately. The noted American sociologist David Riesman denied what seemed Arendt's implication that the totalitarians were acting consistently from the start. She did not do justice to their improvisations, their need to respond to circumstances. Arendt also missed the scope for internal resistance and ended up overdoing the effectiveness of the total domination in the camps, even the possibility of such effectiveness.[46] The influential French social thinker Raymond Aron questioned Arendt's implication that everyone is truly unhappy in a totalitarian regime. And he argued that because Arendt was so convinced of the madness or absurdity of totalitarianism, she neglected the values and purposes of the actors. The Soviet collectivization of agriculture, for example, was not absurd but a plausible quest for higher yields.[47]

To account for motivation, Arendt fastened on ideology, but she did not consider explicitly why anyone would embrace such a totalist ideology, unrealistically positing predictability and denying creativity, in the first place. We can only assume some basis in personality or psychology – perhaps an intolerance for ambiguity, a fear of freedom. In that sense, Arendt, like Popper and Talmon, tended toward reductionism in tracing ideological commitments to personality disorders, thereby avoiding serious engagement with alien ideas.

Peter Baehr charged, convincingly, that Arendt was going overboard in depicting the German people as infused by total terror. Above all, she seemed to contend, without evidence, that the Nazis actually succeeded in atomizing German society. More recent research, Baehr noted, offers little support.[48] More generally, as he saw it, the camps were not remotely an indication of the Nazi relationship with wider German society. Research on participation by ordinary Germans suggests a certain solidarity in complicity with the step-by-step marginalization and dehumanization of German Jews.

But Baehr simply accepts unthinkingly that Arendt shows us how to understand the genesis of the camps and totalitarianism more generally. However compelling her portrayal of the surreality of the camps, she can hardly be the ultimate authority on totalitarianism if she misconstrues the place of the camps in the totalitarian experiment and if her way of depicting German society as infused by total terror does not convince.

It is hardly surprising that subsequent research would open avenues that Arendt did not consider, but it has proven difficult to dislodge the assumption that she nailed the origins and the essence of totalitarianism once and for all. That totalitarianism yielded terrible outcomes is a given. The problem is that Arendt is so seductive that her account diverts us from deeper consideration of how they came to be.

Friedrich and Brzezinski: the political science approach

Prominent among the critics who, finding Arendt's account speculative, called for a more circumspect, empirical approach were Carl J. Friedrich and Zbigniew Brzezinski, who published their *Totalitarian Dictatorship and Autocracy* in 1956. A second edition, with revisions by Friedrich alone, appeared in 1965.

Whereas Arendt was especially concerned with origins, Friedrich and Brzezinski were more concerned with how totalitarianism worked. The various efforts, including Arendt's, to account for origins had proven merely speculative, and thus controversial, because, as Friedrich and Brzezinski saw it, we were not yet prepared actually to *explain* totalitarianism – to explain its genesis, to explain why. So they aimed simply to provide greater precision about this novel form of government, to offer a descriptive model based on generally accepted facts. It was essential, they said, to identify a phenomenon in its full complexity before explanation for its existence could fruitfully be sought.[49] This was classic social science, whereas for Arendt, as we saw, social science was inherently limited as an approach to a unique, unprecedented macro-event like totalitarianism.

Whereas Arendt was concerned with a single macro-process leading to terroristic outcomes, Friedrich and Brzezinski sought to identify commonalities among totalitarian regimes. And, unlike Arendt, they took it for granted that fascist Italy must be included, even as it was obviously less totalitarian in some respects.[50] In the last analysis, the Italian, German, and Soviet regimes were not wholly alike, but they were sufficiently alike, in terms of structure, institutions, and processes of rule, to be classed together and contrasted with others.

Even as Friedrich and Brzezinski departed from Arendt, they gave her credit for grasping the novelty of totalitarianism. These regimes could have arisen only in the context of mass democracy, and they depended on mass legitimation and modern technological means.[51] They differed from earlier instances of tyranny, despotism, or absolutism, terms Friedrich and Brzezinski found highly misleading for the phenomena at issue, though many observers, they charged, missed the distinctions. In the same way, the two authors recognized that whereas past phenomena like ancient Sparta and the medieval monastery bore some superficial resemblances to modern totalitarianism, they did not qualify. And the novelty of modern totalitarianism lay not simply in the quest for total control to mold the whole person, because that effort could be found, for example, in past Muslim and Puritan theocratic regimes.[52]

To encompass such earlier cases, Friedrich and Brzezinski found "totalism" appropriate as the general term. "Autocracy," entailing a characteristic absence of accountability, is another general term that pertains to both earlier and contemporary regimes. Totalitarianism is a specifically modern form of totalism and autocracy, reflecting the advent of new technologies and experience with mass industrial society.[53] At the same time, the two authors convincingly insisted on a sharp distinction between totalitarianism and authoritarianism.

The Friedrich and Brzezinski volume is best known for delineating a classic ideal type of totalitarianism based on six traits:

1 a totalist ideology, covering all aspects of human existence;
2 a single party, typically led by one person; it is a mass party in one sense but includes only a minority, only the most dedicated;
3 a weapons monopoly and thus a monopoly of control over the means of armed combat;

4   a communications monopoly, including control over the means of mass communication made possible by new technologies;

5   terroristic police control, exploiting scientific psychology and directed not only against demonstrable enemies of the regime but also against arbitrarily selected segments of the population;

6   a centrally planned and directed economy.

Together, these six traits form an organic unity; none can be understood in isolation.[54] A weapons monopoly and some measure of centralized economic planning are also found in liberal democratic systems, but again it is the combination that makes for totalitarianism.

Friedrich and Brzezinski usefully emphasized that no complete concentration of power being possible, totalitarianism could only be a matter of degree.[55] And they found limits to "total control" in "islands of separateness," including such spheres as family, religion, and the arts.[56] These were especially hard to penetrate and so limited any totalitarian reach.

Critics found the model in *Totalitarian Dictatorship and Autocracy* too static and mechanical, charging that it missed the revolutionary dynamism of Nazism especially. Friedrich and Brzezinski certainly recognized, however, that the totalitarian regimes were continually evolving.[57] And they usefully characterized, for example, the evolution of the Franco regime in Spain, including its situation by the mid-1950s.[58] In the same way, they noted that changes in the Soviet Union had produced a substantial societal consensus, so that the relatively antagonistic relationship between the Communist Party and society that had emerged under Stalin had given way.[59] In light of Nikita Khrushchev's reforms in the Soviet Union during the later 1950s, Friedrich later came to recognize more explicitly that a totalitarian regime might have greater capacity to evolve than the earlier model had suggested. He even thought it possible that the Soviet Union might abandon totalitarianism altogether, though he still considered it totalitarian in 1965.

On occasion, Friedrich and Brzezinski, like Arendt, seemed to recognize that we cannot understand totalitarianism without probing the totalitarian case against democracy as it had revealed itself in practice. Totalitarian leaders saw theirs as the true democracy, as the fulfillment of democracy, replacing the plutocratic bourgeois version. But the two authors seemed quick to back off, portraying totalitarianism as a mere perversion of democracy, substituting faith for reason and magic exhortation for knowledge and criticism, even as they recognized that some of those negatives could be found in democracies as well.[60]

Robert Jay Lifton and thought reform in communist China

Arendt and Friedrich and Brzezinski have long been considered the classic accounts of totalitarianism, but contributions continued after 1958, often reflecting new concerns. The advent of the communist regimes in China, North Korea, and North Vietnam by the 1950s and the importance of communist movements in Asia and elsewhere intensified concern with phenomena widely considered totalitarian at the time.

The Chinese communist experiment under Mao Zedong in the wake of the revolutionary takeover in 1949 particularly fascinated western observers, not only because of China's geopolitical importance but because the Chinese communists were particularly aggressive in pursuing a totalitarian strategy, very much from the top down, though based on interaction with the masses. Indeed, they seemed to be perfecting techniques that had remained tentative in the hands of their totalitarian predecessors in Europe.

In one of the best known books of the early 1960s, the psychologist Robert Jay Lifton analyzed the effort at thought reform, or "brainwashing," in communist China. We will encounter Lifton's argument again in considering the Chinese communist regime in chapter 4, but in adding to our image of totalitarianism, his study merits inclusion in the present survey. The notion of brainwashing made totalitarianism seem even more sinister, partly because of the implication that all human beings are vulnerable to the techniques being perfected in China.

Prior to doing research for his book, Lifton had taken part in the psychological evaluation of repatriated American soldiers who had been prisoners of war in North Korea during the Korean War. This prompted his subsequent study of people who had undergone "reform" efforts within communist China. He was able to work only with people who, after undergoing such re-education, had opted to leave communist China for Hong Kong. In that sense, he was limited to those who, from the communist perspective, were thought-reform failures. Yet he worked intensively with them and plausibly claimed that his inquiry showed how the Chinese communists operated, thereby helping us understand the successes, limitations, and psychological mechanisms of brainwashing.[61]

Lifton recognized that programs of this sort, entailing imposed dogmas, inquisitions, and mass conversions, could be found in every period, but he insisted that "the Chinese Communists have brought to theirs a more organized, comprehensive, and deliberate – a more *total* – character, as well as a unique blend of energetic and ingenious psychological techniques."[62] Indeed, in Lifton's judgment, Chinese thought reform had "emerged as one of the most powerful efforts at human manipulation ever undertaken."[63] More particularly, the program "has gone far beyond anything their dynastic predecessors or their Russian communist mentors ever attempted."[64]

Lifton took it for granted that in exercising mind control, the leaders were motivated not by power considerations but by their totalist ideology, Marxism-Leninism. But he was concerned primarily with the mechanisms of thought reform. An element of coercion was often involved; most of those who underwent re-education were required to do so. But the technique did not entail overt physical coercion or anything like torture. Lifton wrote: "it was the *combination of external force or coercion* with an appeal to *inner enthusiasm through evangelistic exhortation* which gave thought reform its emotional scope and power."[65] And the key to the conversion experience was group encouragement and pressure.

In this regard, Lifton explicitly compared Chinese practice with Orwell's scenario in *Nineteen Eighty-Four*. Whereas

Orwell envisioned the two-way telescreen as the basic control device, the Chinese achieved greater depth through group experiences in prison or a revolutionary university, which, said Lifton, probably "produce about as thoroughly controlled a group environment as has ever existed." And whereas control of the wider society was less intense, it too was unrivaled in its combination of extensiveness and depth.[66] In another particular, however, Lifton's account suggestively paralleled Orwell's: in the Chinese totalitarian environment, language became restricted, starting with "thought-terminating clichés" like "bourgeois mentality."[67]

Herbert Marcuse and the wider use of totalitarianism

Shortly after the publication of Lifton's book in 1961, the veteran German thinker Herbert Marcuse also tackled totalitarianism, though his angle was diametrically opposed to Lifton's. Emerging from the Frankfurt School of flexible but generally Marxist social criticism, Marcuse left Germany in 1933, soon to settle in the United States. But he maintained close ties with German culture as he became perhaps the single greatest intellectual influence on the New Left of the 1960s and the 1970s on both sides of the Atlantic.

Whereas totalitarianism for Lifton was a dramatic departure from the norms of the open, democratic societies of the West, Marcuse used totalitarianism throughout his widely read *One-Dimensional Man* (1964) to characterize precisely those putatively open, democratic societies, though the source was not so much democracy per se but modern industrial and technological society:

> By virtue of the way it has organized its industrial base, contemporary industrial society tends to be totalitarian. For "totalitarian" is not only a terroristic political coordination of society, but also a non-terroristic economic-technical coordination which operates through the manipulation of needs by vested interests. It thus precludes the emergence of an effective opposition against the whole.[68]

In this society, Marcuse insisted:

> the productive apparatus tends to become totalitarian to the extent to which it determines not only the socially needed occupations, skills, and attitudes, but also individual needs and aspirations. It thus obliterates the opposition between the private and public existence, between individual and social needs. Technology serves to institute new, more effective, and more pleasant forms of social control and social cohesion.[69]

To be sure, the system delivers commodities and entertainments, "but as a good way of life, it militates against qualitative change. Thus there emerges a pattern of *one-dimensional thought and behavior* in which ideas, aspirations, and objectives that, by their content, transcend the established universe of discourse and action are either repelled or reduced to terms of this universe."[70]

Marcuse found a prime example in the dominant modes of linguistic philosophy, which, he insisted, undermined any scope for distancing and critical understanding. We come to accept the wisdom putatively embedded in ordinary language, in everyday usage. Anything outside is mere speculation, fantasy, if not outright nonsense.[71] Such one-dimensionality was inherently totalitarian; no overtly coercive police apparatus was necessary in light of advertising and the inhibiting of critical faculties.

Not that Marcuse was lauding the Soviet Union as an alternative to western democracies. As an industrial society, the Soviet Union was subject to the same totalitarian syndrome. The needs of the modern technology-driven productive system were decisive; any differences over democratic procedures or civil liberties were secondary.[72]

With Marcuse, the focus had shifted from the three earlier regimes to an ongoing tendency in the industrial world, capitalist and communist alike. He remained influential well into the 1970s, and variations on his argument were heard on the Left thereafter, as totalitarianism came up mostly in connection with the "totalizing" potential of modernity, based on instrumental reason.[73] But Marcuse largely fell from view as the context changed over the next several decades. During the 1970s, it became less clear that the modern industrial system could "deliver the goods," though for somewhat different reasons in the western democracies and the Soviet bloc.

And the Soviet bloc began to experience what would prove its terminal structural crisis. Could this be totalitarianism if it could begin to dissipate, unravel? Or did such unraveling entail a deeper revelation of what totalitarianism had meant or might mean?

The testimony of opponents and victims

While still a going concern during the Cold War period, the Soviet bloc attracted considerable attention among those seeking to understand totalitarianism. Even during the 1950s, critical testimony from dissidents like the Pole Czesław Miłosz and the Yugoslav Milovan Djilas, each of whom had experienced communist systems from the inside, illuminated tendencies in totalitarianism that defied earlier understanding. In *The Captive Mind* (1953), Miłosz illuminated modes of resistance and concealment, of thereby maintaining identity, which seemed to indicate limits inherent in totalitarianism. The dynamic he pinpointed, resting on dissimulation above all, seemed an integral aspect of totalitarianism and did not remotely undermine the category.[74] Those he dealt with were specifically totalitarian subjects, but they were not automatons. Rather, they exercised a particular kind of agency. That was an important step beyond Arendt, but those two possibilities – automatons or dissimulation – did not exhaust the modes of distinctively totalitarian experience.

In 1957, Djilas published *The New Class*, showing how the elimination of capitalist ownership in the Soviet Union had not yielded a classless society, as the creators of the Soviet system had genuinely anticipated. Rather, it bred a class never known before, a caste of political bureaucrats enjoying privileges and material advantages, all belying the egalitarian ideology of communism.[75] Orwell had made the same basic point in *Animal Farm*, but Djilas provided an astute analysis of both the unanticipated mechanisms and the implications of the process. Moreover, his experience both as a communist subject and as a dissident, in and out of prison, lent particular credibility to his account.

But it was especially during the 1960s that the testimony of those who had experienced communist totalitarianism firsthand came to enjoy a considerable vogue, which continues to this day. Soviet writers from Alexander Solzhenitsyn to Vassily Grossman and Varlam Shalamov were particularly prominent. Most, like Miłosz and Djilas earlier, had been victims and were deeply critical. And most focused on the "Gulag," an acronym for Main Camp Administration, the Soviet Forced Labor Camp system, which was forged from earlier antecedents in 1931. The term has become virtually synonymous with the violence of Stalinism.[76]

Nikita Khrushchev hinted at the magnitude of the Stalinist terror in his secret speech to a Communist Party congress in 1956, then authorized publication of Solzhenitsyn's *One Day in the Life of Ivan Denisovich* in a Soviet literary magazine in 1962. As an account of an ordinary prisoner's day in a Soviet labor camp of the early 1950s, the story was a watershed, since the repressive nature of the regime had never before been so openly discussed. Solzhenitsyn was already preparing his most influential work, *The Gulag Archipelago*, written in three volumes from 1958 to 1968, though not published until 1973 and then by an émigré Russian publisher in Paris. An English translation followed the next year. The 1973 publication led Solzhenitsyn to be exiled from the Soviet Union.

Only with this work did the term "Gulag" become familiar in the West. *The Gulag Archipelago* was putatively a factual account, and it was indeed based on Solzhenitsyn's own experience as a Gulag prisoner. However, it also included historical analysis and fictional elements. So it was part memoir, part novel, and part historical account, but though the genre was hard to characterize, the combination proved particularly effective.

First in France but then throughout the West, the vogue of Solzhenitsyn helped fuel a reaction among intellectuals against Soviet communism and against what had come to seem a double standard in treatments of communism and fascism. Those who had seemed apologists for the Soviet Union had been too eager to play down its totalitarian character, whether or not by denying any kinship with Nazi Germany. Leading this debunking in France were the so-called New Philosophers, including Bernard-Henri Lévy, André Glucksmann, Alain Finkielkraut, and others. Most had broken with Marxism, having been profoundly influenced by Solzhenitsyn's work.

Meanwhile, cracks in the Soviet satellite states elicited testimony from dissident intellectuals like Adam Michnik in Poland and Václav Havel in Czechoslovakia, who made a quite different contribution to our understanding of totalitarianism. Some of their themes recalled the earlier argument of Czesław Miłosz, but whereas Miłosz considered how people navigated a seemingly intractable totalitarian system, by the 1970s the totalitarianism of the Soviet satellite states seemed to entail a very different dynamic. Though the system remained oppressive, even the leaders no longer seemed to believe in the communist experiment. Everyone was simply going through the motions.

Even as he noted that ideology had long been a mere fig leaf, the British scholar Timothy Garton Ash nicely pinpointed the hollowing at work as he characterized the residual import of ideology in the late phase of communism in the satellite states: "However despised and un-credible these structures of organized lying were, they continued to perform a vital blocking function. They no longer mobilized anyone, but they did prevent the public articulation of shared aspirations and common truths."[77] Moreover, Garton Ash went on, they implicated everyone in a double life of feigned belief, the games of outward conformity. This semantic occupation of the public sphere was all that remained of the earlier energizing commitment and belief.

But Garton Ash saw a way out of this labyrinth in light of the strategy articulated by Havel in "The Power of the Powerless," a widely influential essay of 1978. Havel contended that everyone was both powerful and powerless, both victim and supporter of the system. Individuals behaving *as if* they believed in the system actually became the system, as everyone going through the motions pressured everyone else to do the same. Even making fun of the rituals in private reproduced the official ideology. But thus the apparently powerless had the power to undermine the system simply by ceasing to play the game, performing rituals in which they did not believe, and by living the truth instead.[78]

So much for total control, brainwashed conformity, and the like. But if totalitarianism could evolve in this direction, was the concept worth keeping at all? In fact, it was arguably still meaningful, even essential to understand the distinctive experience and the unforeseen outcome. But it would need to be adjusted to show how totalitarianism could encompass this particular direction, so obviously defying not only original aspirations but the expectations of outside observers.

After the collapse of the Soviet Union and the disintegration of the Soviet bloc, as new documents became available, the reaction against the long-standing defense of the Soviet Union reached something of a culmination with the 1997 publication of a controversial book in French, soon to be translated as *The Black Book of Communism: Crimes, Terror, Repression*, assembled by Stéphane Courtois, Nicolas Werth, and others.[79] They sought to show that Soviet Communism was at least as bad as fascism or Nazism – if anything even worse because it produced more victims.

Plausible though it was, reaction against apologetics for the Soviet Union led, if not to overreaction, at least to moralistic and politicized deflection from the effort to understand more deeply what had gone wrong in the Soviet case. The noted German scholar Karl Dietrich Bracher found it necessary in 1992 to deny that totalitarianism had been a mere Cold War instrument and to insist that it remained indispensable for understanding commonalities between fascist and communist regimes. People in the Soviet bloc, moreover, came widely to accept the category as appropriate to characterize what they were living through – or, once it was over, had lived through. But influential western Leftists like Enzo Traverso and Anson Rabinbach continued to question the category, contending that its use tells us more about those using it than about the historical phenomenon at issue.[80]

Meanwhile, there was also a considerable vogue of Holocaust memoirs, with Primo Levi's perhaps the most influential.[81] Whatever the intentions of the writers, these memoirs helped cement the notion, growing since Arendt, that the Holocaust had revealed the essence of the Nazi system – and, together with the Gulag, of totalitarianism more generally. But Levi and most Holocaust memoirs focused on the experience of the victims and said virtually nothing about how this situation came to be or about the underlying impetus and workings of totalitarianism.

Rather than victimization, however, some featured the courage and humanity, perhaps even "the triumph of the human spirit," which experience of the Holocaust had brought to the fore. Yet any such emphasis on putatively redeeming features incurred the wrath of such major authorities on Holocaust memory as Lawrence Langer and James Young, who insisted that there could be no meaning or redemptive closure, on the one hand, and no "compensatory" cathartic aesthetic pleasure, on the other.[82]

So great was the preoccupation with the Holocaust that by the later 1990s some feared that it was becoming a cliché inviting kitsch. But certainly it evoked serious moral response. As preoccupation continued, resonances were added, so that Tim Cole dared invoke the problematic term "myth" – risky, in light of the persistence of Holocaust denial on the fringes, but plausible, in light of his clear definition and usage. To refer to the "myth" of the Holocaust was not remotely to suggest that it never happened but simply that the "event" itself had to be distinguished from the sort of resonance, evoking strong sentiments and reinforcing basic values, that it had come to have.[83] And especially as "myth," the Holocaust tended to take over our understanding of totalitarianism.

Juxtaposing testimony from both the Soviet Gulag and the Nazi Holocaust raised sensitive but inescapable questions of equivalence, another source of ongoing controversy. Moreover, the juxtaposition further cemented the image of totalitarianism revolving around the extreme outcomes – "the camps," as for Arendt. Privileging the camps to this extent undermined any sense that a broader understanding of totalitarianism was necessary, that even those extreme outcomes could only be understood as products of a wider totalitarian dynamic. Yet, turning in something like the opposite direction, others argued that the camp was the representative institution not only of totalitarianism but of modernity itself.[84] However, such hyperbole provoked outrage among others because it was of course to deny the uniqueness and singularity of the extermination of the Jews. And so it went.

Up to a point, the testimony of opponents and victims surely merits the privilege we tend to accord it. It is often revealing as well as moving. But it can invite moralism, compromising understanding of the wider dynamic.

Christopher Dillon's approach in considering the Nazi concentration camp at Dachau, near Munich, offers a useful alternative angle. Without in any sense minimizing the suffering of those confined there, he showed how Dachau, by now a much-visited German site, seems to feature the experience of the victims to the neglect of how people became torturers and mass murderers at the same place.[85] Dachau proved a key training ground for a cohort of future SS functionaries who would play significant roles in the later program of mass extermination during World War II. Joining others who have turned from psychopathology, obedience, or bureaucratic momentum to account for the brutality at all levels of the camp, Dillon emphasizes commitment and belief. At issue, however, was not some prior, fixed ideology but interplay with the group situation and a particular, newly developing culture, involving certain notions of masculinity and toughness in carrying out tasks that were experienced as extraordinary, heroic, anything but routine.

Moralism and overuse

By the end of the twentieth century, totalitarianism had become central to a family of categories that arguably entailed excessive moralism and politicization, as well as simple overuse. As these tendencies were cresting, they prompted two notable responses, first from the influential Bulgarian-born Parisian intellectual Tzetvan Todorov, then from the Slovenian Slavoj Žižek. We must consider Todorov first as a doubter and critic of the totalitarianism category, but then also as a qualified defender in the next section. Both thinkers grew up in communist eastern Europe, Todorov a defender of liberal democracy, Žižek an innovative Marxist. From these very different angles, each addressed what seemed to be the misuses of totalitarianism and sought to refocus the discussion.

Todorov had already analyzed the Holocaust experience in *Facing the Extreme: Moral Life in the Concentration Camps* (1991), and certainly he appreciated the concern with victims.[86] However, he did not feature victimization per se but the courage and humanity that were brought out. In his *Hope and Memory* (first published in French in 2000), Todorov interspersed an overall interpretation of totalitarianism with essays on notable moral exemplars among survivors of both the Soviet system and the Nazi camps. At the same time, he offered illuminating observations on the tendentious misuse of the past or memory, specifying not simply the need to avoid moralism but also the nature of the appropriately balanced alternative.

Understanding, Todorov insisted, depends to some degree on identification with the perpetrators. We cannot simply dismiss them as madmen or criminals, for there was a logic to what they did. He even proposed that we condemn the sin but pardon the sinner.[87] We must also beware our tendency to make the bad guys always the Other, utterly different from us. And we should refrain from invoking "absolute evil"; totalitarian evil was extreme but not absolute.[88]

Moreover, Todorov criticized what he usefully portrayed as twin ills: on the one hand, the tendency to "sanctify" the past event, especially the Holocaust, making it so ineffable and incomprehensible that we cannot learn from it; on the other hand, the tendency to trivialize the phenomena and the categories at issue through ubiquitous application to the present, as with the endless recourse to Hitler, Nazism, and fascism, which obscures both present and past.[89]

Slavoj Žižek published *Did Somebody Say Totalitarianism? Five Interventions on the (Mis)use of a Notion* in 2001, just a year after Todorov's *Hope and Memory*. But whereas Todorov ended up defending the concept despite all the tendencies toward moralism, Žižek was hostile, charging that relying on totalitarianism relieves us of the duty to think, even keeps us from thinking.[90] Although the Soviet Union was no longer there to be defended, historical understanding still mattered, and lumping it with Nazi Germany obscured the Soviet trajectory, including the reasons for its failure – and thus what was to be learned from it. Marxists especially, said Žižek, should note why the Stalinist purges were more irrational than fascist violence. Paradoxically, the very excess indicates that Stalinism, unlike fascism, was a case of perverted authentic revolution.[91] Moreover, even at its most totalitarian, Stalinist ideology still exuded an emancipatory potential, reflecting a new vision and ethical standard.[92]

So Žižek, like Traverso and Rabinbach, was concerned with political valences, but the reach of his critique of the category was much wider. In adopting his menacing title, *Did Somebody Say Totalitarianism?*, he worried especially about the promiscuous use of this and related categories, making them a kind of smokescreen. He noted, for example, that among the targets of current fears of totalitarianism was "digitalization," portending such ills as the end of privacy. But, he insisted, we misperceive it as a totalitarian threat. And the proper response is not to retreat into the private sphere but to socialize the network since our lives do indeed depend on digitalization, just as they do on the water supply.[93]

Žižek also charged that the totalitarianism category was being used too broadly in radical academia. For the postmodern, deconstructionist Left, "*any* stance that does not endorse the mantra of contingency/displacement/finitude is dismissed as potentially 'totalitarian.'"[94] Later, he contended "that anyone who is not a melancholic, or who does not agree that we are thrown into a contingent finite universe, can today be suspected of 'totalitarianism.'"[95]

In the same vein, Žižek attacked "today's academic Holocaust industry," which tended to make the Holocaust an ineffable enigma, negating all explanations in advance, leaving us with silence. Any attempt to understand the Holocaust historically was taken to be an anti-Semitic negation of its uniqueness. But this stance, Žižek contended, could itself be a mode of political manipulation, whether by aggressive Zionists or by right-wing anti-Semites, undercutting contemporary radical political possibilities. From either side, the charge was that any radical politics portends something like the Holocaust.[96]

Recent defenders and recasters

Even as doubters pulled away or jettisoned the totalitarianism category, some insisted that it remains essential or at least could usefully be recast. Roger Griffin, by then the most influential authority on generic fascism, invoked totalitarianism in taking a fresh look at the relationship between fascism and Marxist communism in a seminal article in 2008. Here he sought to extend his understanding of fascism as revolutionary, wound around myths of redemption and renewal, to the communist revolution, suggesting "a far closer and more uncomfortable affinity between fascism and Soviet or Maoist communism in practice than most Marxists would like to acknowledge." He went on to specify something like the content of the common totalitarianism:

> As forms of political modernism, both offered totalizing solutions to the problem posed by the decadence of liberal society, which were outstanding specimens of the application to sociopolitical engineering of the "historical predictions" that Karl Popper identified with his concept of "historicism" … and with the mainspring of totalitarianism. In both cases, the utopia of a new society was formulated by blending scientific and technological discourse with mythic thinking, thereby producing that characteristic ideological product of modernity, 'scientism'. Both, when implemented, spawned an elaborate 'political religion' and, in their Nazi and Stalinist versions, provided the rationale for mass murder on an industrial scale.[97]

So Griffin was willing to lump fascism and communism as totalitarian partly because of what seemed a common element of political religion. And the renewed interest in political religion by the later 1990s seemed to give the concept of totalitarianism something like a new lease of life. One bit of evidence was the journal *Totalitarian Movements and Political Religions*, launched in 2000. The historians Michael Burleigh and Emilio Gentile (no relation to the earlier philosopher Giovanni Gentile) were particularly instrumental in bringing political religion, understood as a corollary of totalitarianism, to currency.

For Emilio Gentile, in fact, it was especially as new forms of political religion that the three earlier regimes were totalitarian. On that level, fascist Italy was a full participant, even a pioneer.[98] As a political religion, totalitarianism was not a form of rule but an ongoing experiment, animated by the will of the single party, using the state as its instrument. With its characteristic set of dogmas, myths, liturgies, and symbols, the Italian Fascist Party sought at once to create a "new man" and to shape the masses into a single body, dedicated to realizing the party's revolutionary and imperialist aims, which revolved around the creation of a new supranational civilization.

But the relationship between totalitarianism and political religion remained uncertain. Stressing that totalitarianism was not a mere corollary of political religion, Gentile ended up insisting on something like the opposite. Political religion, he argued, is but "one element of totalitarianism, not the principal element and not even the most important in defining its essence." And the nature of totalitarianism itself, he added, "remains a wholly open question."[99]

Even as Tzvetan Todorov usefully delineated some of the pitfalls that had come to surround the totalitarianism category, he insisted that it remained essential. And he nicely pinpointed certain key features, from the accent on toughness to the manipulation of memory and the control of information.[100] But Todorov's defense proved disappointingly conventional, recycling points that had almost become clichés. Such commonplaces are not necessarily wrong, of course; they are simply too easy.

For Todorov, totalitarian ideology was born when three preexisting strands came together: revolutionary ardor (including the use of violence); the millenarian dream of an earthly paradise; and the pseudo-scientific notion that complete knowledge of the human species was about to become available. Totalitarianism required all three.[101]

Elaborating, Todorov noted that totalitarianism was an atheist variant on utopianism and millenarianism. It had its origins in scientism, which seemed to suggest the scope for creating a "new man" through the logic of livestock breeding. And it was no accident that this godless religion prospered in a period marked by the decline of Christianity.[102] Todorov also featured terror, surveillance, the camps, and the totalitarians' simplified division of the world into people to be promoted and people to be eliminated.[103]

This account misconstrued the role of ideology and ended up teleological. As facets of scientism, historical materialism and social Darwinism surely had their place, but Todorov was overinflating their importance, making them "stronger" than they were – or could have been. On that level, even Arendt was more convincing. From her perspective, as we saw, the manifest ideology in the Nazi and Soviet cases was unrealistic, so more was required. However, the "weakness" of the ideology did not lead simply to blind activism, nor did it mean that antecedent ideas played no role. We need to grasp the steps beyond such scientism and the challenges that seemed to open with a new post-developmentalist or anti-determinist sense of history. It did not mean certainty or utopianism but, on the contrary, something more like the anticipation of relentless struggle.

On the basis of the modern cult of science, and Darwinian struggle as one particular corollary, the totalitarians, said Todorov, posited war as the truth of life.[104] But how are we to square such endless struggle with utopianism? Todorov might admit tension from mixing the three ideological strands. However, we also ask how the emphasis on scientific knowledge meshed with the emphasis on will.[105] Todorov at least saw this as an issue, but his way of bringing the strands together looked forced. In the last analysis, his selection of ideological elements seemed arbitrary, and focusing on this tension-ridden agglomeration was simply not very useful. If anything, it merely *seemed* to provide answers when in fact it deflected us from other ways of understanding what had been going on.

As a corollary of his overemphasis on ideology, Todorov, in his section on scientism and humanism, set up the antithesis between totalitarianism and democracy in a Manichean way, as if only humanistic democracy invited continuing experiment, and totalitarianism precluded it.[106] This argument was congruent with Karl Popper's, but it missed the totalitarian sense of the need and scope for experiment, for making history in a new way, in light of the possibilities that emerged in the wake of the Great War.

Given these grounds for doubt, Todorov's neglect of the Italian case proved especially damaging. Italian fascism did not reject modern science, but its fundamental thrust was idealist and anti-materialist, though the Italians, too, aimed to produce a "new man" through totalitarian mobilization and education. On that basis, as we will see in the next chapter, the Italian fascist mainstream would claim superiority over Nazism and Soviet communism, both taken as crudely materialistic.

In discussing freedom, incompleteness, and unforeseeability, making for ever new challenges, Todorov plausibly valued humanism over totalism and scientism.[107] But humanism encompasses the totalitarian fascist Giovanni Gentile, whose thinking was far from scientism, and who, as we noted, posited a radical form of human freedom and responsibility. Obviously, there is a symptomatic difference between Gentile's totalitarian humanism and Todorov's democratic humanism, but Todorov's categories keep us from even asking about its basis.

A few years after Todorov's book was published, I offered my own recasting of totalitarianism, focusing on the three classic regimes, in *The Totalitarian Experiment in Twentieth-Century Europe* (2006).[108] To establish the background, I rethought much of Arendt's still useful argument concerning rights, interests, political virtue, and the requirements for a systematic alternative to the mainstream liberal order. I also treated intellectual antecedents, focusing not directly on Marxism and social Darwinism but partly on offshoots of each – on the one hand, the turn-of-the-century revision of Marxism and, on the other, eugenics, the putatively scientific effort to improve the human "stock," especially to enhance the competitiveness of some particular country. Each of these currents posited the need and scope for new modes of human agency beyond quasi-deterministic nineteenth-century ideologies. I also found a key role for Giovanni Gentile.

Writing six years later, Richard Shorten treated my book with respect in his *Modernism and Totalitarianism* (2012), but he thought I was missing sight of the wood for the trees.[109] This was apparently because he demanded an approach even more overtly teleological than Arendt's or Todorov's. Moreover, whereas Todorov sought to box out moralism, Shorten's teleological approach was unapologetically moralistic. He insisted that the long-standing structural model, focusing on how totalitarian regimes worked, "needs to be superseded by what might be described as the 'genocidal model,'" starting with the most extreme, genocidal outcomes. Such privilege to mass murder "resonates with generally prevalent moral intuitions regarding what it was that was really specific to the Nazi and Stalinist episodes in the twentieth century."[110] Indeed, Shorten argued, "what justifies the addition of a new word to the political lexicon is the experience of political mass murder, being sponsored by the leadership of a modern state, and being exceptional in both intention and scale."[111]

As Shorten saw it, focusing on the murderous outcomes made clear the importance of ideology, which he delineated in three strands, much like Todorov's: utopianism, scientism, and revolutionary violence. Each had to do with creating a "new man," and it was this underlying commitment to anthropological revolution that gave coherence to the ideology.[112] These elements are all widely emphasized, and each undeniably had some place in the mix. But each is vague, and Shorten's teleological model led him to overemphasize and force them, thereby precluding other angles on the same evidence.

In treating Soviet utopianism, for example, Shorten started with Marx but noted some shifting of gears with Stalin and the embrace of "socialism in one country" as the goal: "'Socialism in one country' pictured, as utopia's collective subject, not so much the proletariat per se as the *Russian* proletariat."[113] For Shorten, that was simply to change the utopia's terms, not to abandon or postpone it. But how Marxian utopianism played out within Stalinism is not so clear. What would it take for Shorten to concede that the original utopianism had given way to something else with different sources and implications? Having posited utopianism as one of the three central facets up front, he seemed determined to frame whatever resulted as a mere variant on utopianism, thereby precluding the possibility of anything else. A more deeply historical treatment, with more attention to the secret doubts among Soviet leaders, the sense that they were in risky uncharted territory and could only improvise, might point in a different direction.

In the same way, Shorten recognized that "in races Nazism had crucial collective units, though ... not quite a racial determinism, since at no point in Nazi thought is the triumph of one race over others pictured as being inevitable in advance."[114] Shorten went on to add: "As Nazi thought made clear, 'laws of Nature' did not operate independently of human will. They had to be applied."[115] He also noted that Hitler "gives a definition of politics that suggests that a racial theory of history does not arrive at its terminus – the victory of the stronger race – independently of human action: 'politics is ... the implementation of a nation's struggle for existence.'"[116] Indeed, Hitler worried that a historical destiny might well elude a people in the absence of an active will to enact that destiny.

What did all this say about the relative importance of science and whatever the "post-ideological" admixture that kept the Nazis going, that motivated them, in light of the *lack* of any deterministic scientistic assurance? Darwinism surely affected their sense of possibilities and priorities, but insofar as the "laws of nature" had to be applied by human beings, they were not really laws at all. Neither Darwin, nor scientism more generally, could tell them how to marshal energies and mobilize for the collective action necessary. Hitler's concern that a historical destiny might elude a people suggested that the measure of superiority was not only, perhaps not even primarily, race but the capacity to come together and act collectively to enact that destiny. It might have been the next step that made the course of action specifically totalitarian.

Although Todorov simply ignored the Italian case, Shorten explicitly excluded Italy and offered a cogent explanation. For one thing, the Italian trajectory did not yield the same genocidal outcome.[117] But even more important was Shorten's reading of the Nazis' rejection of the putative statism of fascist Italy, the syndrome we considered earlier in this chapter. Whereas, as we saw, the Nazis were perfectly willing to call the Italians totalitarians on that basis, for Shorten it meant that fascist Italy could not have been totalitarian. Race for Nazism and social class for Stalinism provided powerful constructions of social identity; the 'state' could never have played a comparable totalitarian role.[118]

As we noted earlier, the state/*Volk* divide between Italy and Germany is significant, but it is not grounds for portraying one as totalitarian and the other not. And in any case, though Italian totalitarianism indeed featured the state, the Italian fascists often discussed the nation or the people and its relationship with the state. And how to conceive that relationship provoked major disagreements. But this was disagreement among totalitarians about how best to conceive the relationship between state and people beyond liberal democracy.

It was not the genocidal outcome that warranted adding the term "totalitarianism" to our vocabulary; Shorten simply falls into teleological moralism in insisting on that justification. The rejection of liberal democracy and the quest for a systematic alternative is what first demands our attention. At the time, as I have emphasized, some found the totalitarian novelty in both theory and practice promising, but it yielded many unanticipated outcomes, some genuinely horrific. By now, it is the whole package that demands our attention.

3

Totalitarian Trajectories During the Era of the Two World Wars

Recasting the category

Grasping the limits of the mainstream accounts suggests how the totalitarianism category might fruitfully be recast, first as an approach to fascist Italy, the Soviet Union, and Nazi Germany, the regimes to which it was first applied. The keys are to avoid the teleological bias and the overemphasis on preexisting ideologies that we found in several influential analyses.

Rather than start with outcomes, as if each departure had some built-in goal, we need a genetic approach, pondering aspirations in light of context. This requires considering the scope for new departures in the wake of the expectation-defying upheavals surrounding World War I and the Russian Revolution. Particular circumstances in Russia, Italy, and Germany enhanced the sense of challenge and extraordinary yet transitory opportunity. For somewhat different reasons in each, it seemed possible, and necessary, to move to the forefront, leapfrogging the liberal democracies. The Russian Revolution inspired Mussolini, Mussolini inspired Hitler, and the three regimes fed on each other thereafter in this age of new possibility. Each was an open-ended experiment, subject to contingencies, though in retrospect we recognize the scope for terrible outcomes.

During the late nineteenth century, Marxism and social Darwinism involved elements of determinism, specifying a definite direction, but, by the early twentieth, history had come to seem, even to many adherents to those ideologies, more open-ended and uncertain, more the product of contingent choices by living human beings. So those prior ideologies only carried so far. Totalitarianism is best understood not as a means to implement a prior ideology but as a further, historically specific step beyond determinism, as an effort to master that history. Although Hannah Arendt and Richard Shorten had a general sense that something beyond ideology required explanation, what each offered was still relatively conventional. Neither seriously pondered how and why the totalitarians more radically worked beyond those original ideologies – or the implications of their having done so.

Something like a mentality or frame of mind was surely at work, but it was post-ideological. In their different ways, such figures as Friedrich Nietzsche, Georges Sorel, Vilfredo Pareto, and Lenin himself had earlier suggested that a new, extraordinary mode of action had become necessary precisely because history was more contingent upon human will, spirit, organization, and collective action, than had previously been recognized. As open and uncertain, it required improvisation and might depend on myth, an overused category to be unpacked later in this chapter. Totalitarianism usefully characterizes that new mode of collective action.

We find in the early totalitarian departures a certain hubris, but it stemmed less from a claim to a privileged grasp of the direction of history than from a sense of having discerned, as the mainstream liberals and orthodox Marxists had not, the requirements for the new, history-making mode of action itself. Still, uncertainty shadowed the confidence. So mixed characteristically with hubris was a certain shrillness, reflecting the *lack* of any suprahistorical assurance, the feeling that it was all up to them, fallible human beings acting within an unforeseeable history.

To meet the challenge and seize the historical moment seemed to require concentrating power and mobilizing populations to make possible the grandiose collective action necessary. Thus, most basically, the role of the single party but also the hypertrophy of the state. Relations between the party and the state varied, but the aim was to create a more effective society and even a superior mode of human self-realization, not simply to dominate totally, to turn people into automatons, or to maintain power.

As a departure from liberalism and individualism, this would entail an expansion of the public sphere, including the sovereignty of the state, in principle without limit, at the expense of the private. In each case, such expansion included, as a particularly telling example, a measure of population engineering and an emphasis on the public implications of once-private choices in the population sphere. To get married and have children was now inherently political, indeed, a form of political participation. As the reverse side of the expansion of sovereignty, people were to be involved through more constant and direct participation, again in principle without limit.

Ordinary people got caught up in these experiments in ways that we have only recently begun to understand. It was not only, or even primarily, through coercion, fear, terror, or even conformity, though the totalitarianism category long suggested something along those lines. In participating, doing their part, some ordinary people felt an energizing sense of involvement in something extraordinary, unprecedented, even beyond conventional notions of good and evil.

The extraordinariness of the situation seemed to mandate the use of violence on occasion, though modes of violence varied considerably. We find political police in each of the three cases, and there was surely a period of terror in the Soviet Union during the 1930s, as we will discuss below. But generalized terror, as posited by Arendt, was never central in any of the three, and by now most authorities have come to play it down apart from targeted groups.

In all three countries, a self-proclaimed new elite achieved a monopoly of power on the basis of its claim to be uniquely qualified to spearhead the post-democratic form of collective action necessary. What the three regimes actually set out to do by means of the totalitarian mode of action varied, but, in all three cases, the new action produced a characteristic dynamic, sometimes including impressive results.

However, it also entailed exaggeration, rhetorical overkill, and mythical thinking – thinking that was energizing up to a point but that blinded those involved to their real prospects. Partly as a result, the dynamic proved to occasion overreach and all manner of unintended consequences, including, most basically, a tendency to spin out of control. That tendency does not mean that these phenomena were not totalitarian after all; it was simply one aspect of what, as it turned out, totalitarianism could involve.

In each of the three, the totalitarian dynamic resulted in certain common features, from narrowing into truncated modes of participation to a tendency toward partly out-of-control radicalization, which could include mass killing. The contracting toward personal dictatorship in all three cases was but an outcome of the totalitarian dynamic, not an indication of originating intentions, not evidence that it all boiled down to mere personal dictatorship all along. And we must view even the most terrible outcomes in terms of particular contingent trajectories, rather than simply posit evil or ideological fanaticism up front. These outcomes followed from the novel totalitarian mode of action itself.

Some of the reasons for doubt adduced by critics do not undermine but support such a recast use of the category. This is true of Richard Overy in his study of Hitler's Germany and Stalin's Russia, even as he suggests that totalitarianism is a "political-science fantasy" best jettisoned altogether.[1] And the contributors to Michael Geyer and Sheila Fitzpatrick's *Beyond Totalitarianism* are so determined to undermine the earlier model, featuring putatively totalitarian commonalities between Nazi Germany and the Soviet Union, that they underplay other similarities suggesting the scope for recasting totalitarianism.[2] Indeed, the Geyer–Fitzpatrick volume is especially useful in showing how the new totalitarian mode of action triggered overreach and excess, yet also new modes of initiative from below. And it shows how interaction fed the extremism of both the Nazis and the Soviets. The sense that they were doing the same grandiose, history-making kind of thing was comparably energizing in each case and comparably fed a tendency toward out-of-control excess. So the results of this pioneering research point not "beyond totalitarianism" but only beyond the earlier, largely discredited version – and help us conceive the alternative.

As one aspect of leapfrogging the liberal democracies, each of the three regimes envisioned recasting the present world order seemingly controlled by the western imperialist powers, who seemed to be promoting liberal democracy in their own interests. In their different ways, the fascists and communists claimed to offer a systematic alternative. But despite such commonalities, the three early regimes were also rivals, competing for the post-liberal space, feeding on each other as they did so. The rivalry between the fascist powers and the Soviet Union comes first to mind, but fascist Italy and Nazi Germany were also rivals, even as comrades in the crusade against communism.

Fascist Italy

We have seen that many authorities exclude fascist Italy from the totalitarian universe. Arendt and Shorten explicitly precluded it for essentially the same reasons: on the one hand, its lack of a terroristic apparatus and genocidal outcome; on the other, its apparently conservative statism.

In addition, the fascist regime was a "dyarchy," with King Victor Emmanuel III remaining in place throughout Mussolini's tenure. The dyarchy notion, writ large, has long seemed to suggest Mussolini's overall compromise with pre-fascist elites and institutions. In the same way, the arrangements with the Catholic Church reached with the Concordat and the Lateran Pacts of 1929 have seemed the archetypal indication that any radical, totalitarian thrust in fascism got bogged down.

But our concern with aspirations, as well as with practice, functioning, and outcomes, must especially be kept in mind in approaching the Italian case. The Italian fascists wanted and claimed to be totalitarian, so any consideration of totalitarianism in its genesis would have to ask what they were seeking and why. In recent years, there have been significant though contrasting efforts to reincorporate the Italian case, even in the face of obvious differences with Nazi Germany and the Soviet Union. The most prominent has been that of Emilio Gentile, who warned against measuring fascist Italy against some Hollywood version or abstract standard. As simply "the Italian way to totalitarianism," Italian fascism produced a regime that was not qualitatively different from the Nazi and Stalinist regimes.[3] But as we noted in chapter 2, Gentile emphasized political religion – liturgy, ritual, the "sacralization of politics" – and argued for the inclusion of Italy largely on that basis. Whereas ritual and liturgy must be considered, it is not necessary to feature political religion to make the case for including fascist Italy. Indeed, Gentile's categories deflect us from a deeper array of questions about the sources and implications of the totalitarian aspiration in the Italian case.

Let us address two of the grounds for doubt more explicitly. How much difference did the presence of preexisting elites and institutions actually make? As opposed to taming "genuine" fascism, as has so often been assumed, they were often co-opted, even caught up in synergy with the novel fascist thrust. The presence of fascism, with its totalitarian aspirations, drew in elements from the prior elites and institutions and led them to play roles they could not have played under the liberal regime. As one example, the *Istituto per la ricostruzione industriale* (Institute for Industrial Reconstruction, or IRI) was created first as an ad hoc response to the Depression, not as a specifically fascist measure. But from within the fascist framework it quickly became a vehicle for the statist management of major sectors of the economy. Thus the business magnate Arturo Beneduce found an opportunity to play a statist economic role that he could not have performed, and never sought to perform, under the preceding liberal regime.

Certainly, the Concordat of 1929, giving the Catholic Church a role in education and in marriage law, seems utterly untotalitarian on the face of it. But that did not settle the regime's relationship with the Church. Those measures greatly displeased many fascists, who sought a more consistently totalitarian policy. Partly in response, Mussolini turned back toward militancy with a crack-down on the Church's youth organization, Catholic Action, in 1931. Establishing a monopoly over the formation of Italian youth remained a major preoccupation for Mussolini and leading fascists.

Meanwhile, Pope Pius XI issued encyclicals in 1930 and 1931 criticizing fascist family and welfare policy, especially the fascist effort to politicize marriage and childrearing and to secularize Catholic organizations helping the poor and sick. Another encyclical, *Non abbiamo bisogno*, went further to denounce, as pagan idolatry, the very notion of the totalitarian state. So friction continued, though by the eve of World War II the regime was, on balance, expanding its reach at the expense of the Church.

What about the putative statism of fascist Italy? The emphasis on codified law especially reflected the vision of minister of justice Alfredo Rocco. Though his conception surely contrasted with the Nazi emphasis on dynamism and will, his approach shows that totalitarianism can be legal and even legally mandated. The law might be enforced entirely predictably and even-handedly in a totalitarian system.

In any case, important though he was, Rocco did not speak for all Italian fascists; such leading intellectuals as Giovanni Gentile and Camillo Pellizzi, in trumpeting Italy's totalitarian ethical state, offered a much more dynamic and open-ended conception. As a way of adapting to the seeming open-endedness of history, the totalitarian state was never to be finished once and for all, fulfilled in some set of empirical institutions; it was constantly to be recreated as the state tackles ever-new tasks and as new generations come to political consciousness through education and experience.[4] Any notion that the Italian totalitarian ideal, as statist, had to require static subservience to codified law was based on a selective, tendentious reading of the evidence.

Nonetheless, the relationship between the Fascist Party and the state has been hard to pin down. The Fascist Grand Council was transformed from a party into a state institution in 1928, but was this to tame the party or revolutionize the state? It was some of both, but it was more to fascistize the state, and a clearly totalitarian measure, diminishing the bifurcation between party and state. It was not remotely the same as the preexisting liberal state absorbing a fascist party entity.

But dispute about the relationship between party and state persisted throughout the course of the regime, and confusion about what constituted radical or genuinely totalitarian fascism has led to persistent misconstrual of the stakes. Often the party is taken as embodying radical fascism, so those seeking to tame or delimit the party are assumed to have been merely conservative, not totalitarian. Such fascists were more likely to favor legal methods and moderate tactics, but for many subordinating the party did not remotely mean ending the fascist revolution and returning to normal. The long-standing tendency to associate the revolutionary, totalitarian potential of fascism with party radicals like Roberto Farinacci has severely restricted understanding of the elements in play.

But why did the fascists find it necessary to break from the liberal democratic mainstream in the first place, and why did they actually aspire to a totalitarian alternative? Among those on their way to fascism in Italy, something like a totalitarian ideal was becoming almost explicit around the end of World War I, before the fascist movement was formed and before the term "totalitarianism" was coined. Indeed, it was evident in disaffected elements coming from both Left and Right. Their proposals responded to the widespread sense that the Italian liberal parliamentary state was too weak to confront the challenges of the immediate postwar period, especially trade union militancy, which included public service strikes and even factory occupations. Liberalism seemed to portend endless class conflict.

Even some on the Right who saw the unions as a threat from within the permissive liberal order recognized that they had played a positive role – in providing an antidote to atomization, in raising the consciousness of the workers, and in nurturing such virtues as collaboration, discipline, and self-sacrifice. In the liberal context, they threatened particularism and disruption, but they might play a further positive role from within a different political framework. In the context of Italy's postwar crisis, and before Mussolini became prime minster in October 1922, there was much debate over how to take advantage of the positives and to eliminate the negatives of the trade union phenomenon, especially by integrating working-class formations into a wider corporatist structure organizing all sectors of production.

These economically based groupings would no longer be private entities, like the existing unions, but would become mandatory public entities, exercising public functions. Entities based on economic roles might even provide the basis for a healthier, more productive alternative to parliamentary government and the multiparty system.[5] This was a totalitarian direction, but such a departure from liberal democracy could seem rational, benign, and progressive. The unions were attractive not simply as a means of manipulation or control. Nor did the vision have anything to do with torture or violence, let alone with total domination, reducing individuals to automatons. But it entailed mandatory participation; everyone would have to get on board. So even as Italian fascism lacked an ideology like Marxism or Social Darwinism, it had from the outset some ideas about how to build a post-liberal order, one that might be considered totalitarian.

Although accents varied among fascists, Italian fascism rested not on the earlier ideological certainties but on a wider humanism featuring the scope for positive mobilization and inclusiveness based on education, culture, and the ethical capacity that pertained to human beings. For human beings were neither automatons nor necessarily subject to materialistic, mechanical limits based on class or race. Giovanni Gentile's thinking, considered in the preceding chapter, was central to this notion.

This overall idealism, or emphasis on spirit, encompassed a new sense, itself energizing, that grandiose achievement could be fueled by concentrating power, mobilizing people, and organizing for energetic collective action around commitment, audacity, will, solidarity, faith, discipline, sacrifice, and something like myth, a category that the Italians embraced explicitly. But myth is a slippery and overloaded category that must be treated with particular care. The fascist embrace of myth may seem to suggest mystification, cynical manipulation from above – to serve the interests of the elite, diverting the masses from their real interests.

In fact, myth was implicated in Italian fascism on several levels, with proportions and even meanings changing over time. But as embraced by the creators of fascism, myth did not differentiate elites from masses but bound them together, for even the new fascist elite knew itself to be caught up in an overall myth as it pursued ongoing fascist creation. Writing in 1934, a leading ideologue, Giuseppe Bottai, noted that fascism was widely seen abroad as a doctrine of myths but, turning the tables, he insisted that the liberal mainstream had come to venerate liberty and the individual precisely as idols, myths.[6] The point, however, was not simply that two can play this game. The fascists claimed a more lucid grasp of the place of myth as central to a new historical-political sense that could itself *change* how history happens, or gets made, by projecting heroic collective goals wound around images of collective accomplishment.

Even as they talked explicitly in terms of myths, leading early fascists like Dino Grandi insisted that the new mode of action had to produce concrete institutional change, that mere mobilization through myth was not sufficient. And certainly the fascists embarked on a concerted program of institutional change, with corporatism as the centerpiece. But the most basic priority was simply energetic action, and in that sense the long-standing imputation of "activism" to Italian fascism is close to the mark. The point, however, was not simply to "keep the masses in motion" but to accomplish things, to show what could be accomplished through the energizing new mode of collective action.

Totalitarianism expressed the regime's determination to mold a new Italian, to shape a new society, to make Italy great and powerful. Mussolini famously boasted in 1927 that fascism would "make Italy unrecognizable to itself and to foreigners in ten years."[7] This was to be the basic totalitarian project in Italy, and it meant that in principle Fascism was prepared to take on anything and everything. In that spirit, the regime embraced an array of mobilizing great tasks, often characterized through military metaphors, from the reconstruction of the Italian infrastructure to the battles for grain, on the one hand, and for births, on the other. The "battle for births" was central to fascist demographic policy, which was less radical than Nazi Germany's but comparably totalitarian. As opposed to eugenics, the Italians emphasized natalism, encouraging population growth, and the battle included a good deal of public health and welfare legislation to foster healthy mothers and children.

The sense of being caught up in grand and unprecedented collective action seems to have captured the imaginations of ordinary Italians up to a point. But totalitarianism meant, quite explicitly, that there was no room for political indifference; anyone who was not actively for fascism was against it. It also meant the expansion of state sovereignty. Speaking in October 1925, Mussolini offered perhaps his best-known dictum: "Our formula is this: everything within the state, nothing outside the state, no one against the state."[8]

At the same time, virtually from the start, the fascists began organizing and indoctrinating the population. Indeed, although they learned from socialist examples, they quickly pushed the effort to unprecedented levels, partly through the pioneering use of new media. As early as 1923, Mussolini proclaimed cinema to be fascism's strongest weapon. Although commemorative exhibitions and various forms of spectacle became still more central during the 1930s, ritual and commemoration were significant from the start. Moreover, almost at once the fascists began mobilizing and politicizing Italians through organizations for women, for youth, for university students, and, with the *Opera Nazionale Dopolavoro*, for leisure time.

The central vehicle for mobilization, education, and participation was the corporatist system, intended to politicize economic roles and the workplace in what was to be a society of producers, without "parasites." Occupational groupings were to provide a more productive basis for political involvement, as people came to understand the political implications of their own economic roles and as they shared in the expanded range of decisions to be made politically through the corporative entities. At the same time, corporatism encompassed the whole sphere of labor relations, which had come to seem increasingly problematic under liberal democracy, but which now could be managed more effectively through the totalitarian state. In principle, the corporatist direction was at once to expand the sovereignty of the state, politicizing the economy, and to mobilize people more constantly and directly through their roles as producers.

After the fact, the corporatist system was long marginalized in discussions of fascist Italy because, despite significant legislation and institutional change, it did not live up to its considerable fanfare. But it was central to the fascist self-understanding as at once hypermodern and totalitarian, and especially before the regime's turn to overt imperialism in 1935, it was widely seen, in Italy and abroad, as the center-piece of Italian fascism.

In the last analysis, we find in fascist Italy grandiose ambition and rhetoric, some significant initiatives and achievements, but also much frustration and failure reflecting the overreach that proved typical of the early totalitarian experiments. Even by the early 1930s, the overall effort in Italy was encountering frustration, a sense of blunting and impasse. Achievement constantly fell short of the rhetoric that surrounded every initiative. Partly because of funding limita-tions, even the new welfare legislation was generally poorly implemented. By the early 1930s, an array of committed fascists had become sharply and openly critical of the devel-oping corporatist institutions, which tended to function in a top-down way, precluding autonomy and initiative. The new system suffered from institutional rivalries, bureaucratic meddling, business opposition, and disagreement over the relative importance of discipline and initiatives from below.

Such disagreements over corporatism provide a prime example of the debilitating fissuring that was barely concealed beneath the facade of monolithic unity. We note comparable fissuring over the respective roles of the Fascist Party and the state – the totalitarian corporate state. Quite apart from the inevitable personal rivalries and careerism, the very effort to act in the new way added layers of scapegoating in light of unanticipated difficulties and unintended outcomes. As the initial thrust blunted, the stylistic dimension became more central, even tended to take on a life of its own, as if ritual and spectacle themselves constituted post-liberal participation.

The cult of the *Duce* of the 1930s, summed up in the fatuous slogan "Mussolini is always right," was an aspect of the narrowing and trivialization in course. The deepening reliance on the leader invited capriciousness as Mussolini grew increasingly mistrustful and isolated. Unwilling to delegate, he sought to juggle too many functions and ended up making decisions impulsively without adequate preparation.

A sense that fascism was in danger of getting bogged down in compromise and infighting helped fuel the emphasis on foreign affairs that led to the imperialist conquest of Ethiopia (Abyssinia) in 1935–6, then to intervention in the Spanish Civil War, to the Axis alliance with Nazi Germany, and to intervention in World War II. Even those otherwise skeptical that fascism was totalitarian have tended to recognize a developing totalitarian thrust surrounding this turn, which led to militarization, an anti-bourgeois "reform of custom," and anti-Semitic legislation on the domestic level. But these were outcomes of the dynamic in course, not a revelation of original purposes.

Although in principle the logic of totalitarian practice might have suggested eliminating Jewish separateness altogether, anti-Semitism did not figure prominently in Italian fascism until the later 1930s. In fact, Jews were slightly more than proportionally represented in fascism, and many Jews welcomed fascist governmental measures in the early 1930s that seemed to regularize their status as a national minority. It has increasingly become clear that the turn to anti-Semitism by 1938 did not stem from German pressures. So why? The presence of the Jews as a somewhat distinctive community had nothing to do with the difficulties of acting in the totalitarian way envisioned, but in light of the very real obstacles, the internal fragmentation and ambiguity, the fascists could do no better than to fasten onto this bogus issue as they sought to rekindle the fascist revolution.

Even as they grumbled and criticized, the fascists' self-understanding became ever more mythical as they faced competition from Nazi Germany and even as radicalization yielded trivialization. Thus they overstated both actual achievements and continued prospects. Although the sense of Italian difference and leadership continued to inspire, its inflating mythical dimension increasingly blinded the fascists to reality. In fact, the fascist revolution itself became a myth. It only seems paradoxical to insist that the outcomes of Italian fascism were quintessentially totalitarian even as, precisely as, they made a mockery of the regime's totalitarian pretenses.

The communist experiment in the Soviet Union

The Bolsheviks, a minority within the wider Russian socialist movement, managed to take over the country in the complex revolution of 1917. Earlier, their leader, Vladimir Lenin, had fashioned a distinctive variant within European Marxism, specifying a particular leadership role for a minority party, "the vanguard of the proletariat," based on consciousness, will, and organization. But the aim was not a mere coup d'état from above. Lenin envisioned synergy with a popular uprising, which the vanguard party, based on its privileged grasp of Marxism, would know how to recognize and channel into productive action.

Shortly after taking power, the Bolsheviks relabeled themselves communists, then, in 1919, claimed leadership over the world Marxist movement in founding the Third (or Communist) International, widely known as the Comintern. In 1922, they changed the name of the country from Russia to the Union of Soviet Socialist Republics (USSR, or Soviet Union), after the soviets, or councils, that had been central to the revolution in 1917.

To attempt such a revolution in a relatively backward country defied Marxist orthodoxy, but Lenin had insisted that, in the context of a major European war, revolution in Russia could spark wider European revolution. The Russians would not be left to go it alone. The spread of revolution seemed possible into 1920, as revolutionary unrest gripped much of Europe, but by 1921 the wave clearly had ended, at least for the foreseeable future.

Still, the communists had made a revolution, and made it stick by winning the civil war that followed from 1918 to 1920. Each was a considerable achievement, breeding confidence. But those successes rested not on the validity of Marxism but on the seeming effectiveness of Leninism itself, based on a capacity to act in light of a putatively privileged consciousness, will, and capacity for organization. Even as orthodox Marxism was being strained, however, the communists clung to it, with its promise of universal relevance and its assurance that history was on their side. But as they proceeded, following a certain mode of action, they diverged ever further from orthodoxy. The course from there rested less on Marxism than on the logic of this particular mode of action, on their capacity to organize and act in the appropriate new way.

Even as the communists continued to invoke the ideology, it became ever more elastic, even contradictory. Marxist class categories remained central, but their use was variable, then blurred. "Bourgeois" came to mean opposition or deviation; that opposition or deviance was "bourgeois" was true a priori. The variable factor had nothing to do with the differentiated socioeconomic roles that had led Marx to posit class as determinant; rather, the variable factor encompassed consciousness, belief, commitment, will.

Claims of Marxist orthodoxy masked only superficially the sense of vulnerability and vertigo that the communist venture entailed. Isolated in a relatively backward country, torn by World War I and then civil war, surrounded by hostile or potentially hostile countries, they faced unprecedented challenges. The difficulties of action led to the use of military metaphors – and even self-understanding in military terms. Among the essential virtues required were toughness and pitilessness. Yet even if they were more radically departing from Marxism than they wanted to recognize, the opportunity to create a new, post-bourgeois order was genuine. So what was to be done?

Lenin died early in 1924 after a series of strokes, and the ensuing struggle over the leadership was inevitably bound up with controversy over priorities in this unforeseen situation. Joseph Stalin gradually emerged as the winner by the later 1920s. Although the Soviets continued to promote an international communist movement, they set out under Stalin to build "socialism in one country." But what that meant and how to proceed were by no means clear, so there were many fits and starts. In 1927, eagerness to rekindle the revolution after a period of retrenchment led to the adoption of full-scale economic planning, which up to a point was modeled on the German effort that had intrigued Lenin during World War I. But the Soviet enterprise was unprecedented in ambition and magnitude. The advent of planning elicited much enthusiasm; not only would Russia be propelled out of backwardness but it would show the world, for the first time, the scope for human mastery of the economy. And the planning enterprise attracted widespread attention abroad.

Then came Stalin's decision, by the end of 1929, for crash industrialization based on forced collectivization in agriculture. It was reckless, but the feeling was that it could be done through will, enthusiasm, and heroic effort. In his speech of December 1929 announcing the policy shift in agriculture, Stalin indicated that the kulaks, relatively prosperous peasant landowners, were to be liquidated as a class. So rather than merely having their property expropriated, the kulaks were often killed or sent to forced labor camps. Now the camp system – the Gulag – reached gigantic proportions, gradually assuming a major role in the economy. But the industrialization effort galvanized great enthusiasm, especially as competition with the two fascist regimes heated up and as the liberal democratic mainstream became mired in depression.

The effort was experienced not simply as catch-up, overcoming relative backwardness. Crash industrialization, guided by central planning and without private profit, was understood by leaders and led alike as the great task of "building socialism," though there was no claim that they had actually achieved it. Indeed, *building* socialism seemed to require virtues different from, even antithetical to, socialist egalitarianism. With labor quality emphasized, workers were encouraged to compete for rewards, and a cult developed around heroic workers who exceeded their quotas. Differentiation seemed legitimate because it was functional, essential to the great task they were all carrying out together. And the sense of building socialism was essential to the energizing sense of wider mission, of showing the world a morally superior modern society, without exploitation, based on planning, and spreading benefits from health care to paid vacations.

However, the overall effort was rash, more than the leaders could handle, and thus produced unintended negative consequences. The enthusiasm itself, the sense that they were accomplishing miracles, bred inflated claims and unrealistic production targets. The tendency to exaggerate achievements made expectations even more unrealistic. Because they were determined to move so fast, many of those entrusted with managerial positions in the planned economy were simply unprepared. The resulting incompetence invited compensating corruption, drunkenness, or heavy-handedness in dealing with workers. At the same time, the leadership encouraged denunciations from below against plant managers and supervisors. Ordinary workers were often eager to comply, feeling they were furthering the cause of building socialism, even as they may have been settling scores at the same time.

However, the competition among workers, leading to strongly differential rewards, ended up sapping the enthusiasm it initially inspired. Moreover, solicitude for individual achievement did not mesh with the orderly procedure and predictability necessary for sustainable increases in production.

Systematic opposition to the Stalinist direction began to surface especially in 1932. Moreover, beginning in 1933, when Hitler came to power, the Soviet Union faced significant international threats from Germany and, increasingly, imperial Japan. Leon Trotsky, one of Stalin's major rivals for the leadership, had been exiled in 1929 and remained a potential rallying point for others disillusioned with the Stalinist course. The combination of genuine enemies and domestic overreach bred a sense of crisis and vulnerability alongside the continuing enthusiasm and sense of extraordinary achievement. The encouragement of denunciations from below, the intensified suspicion, and the accusations of sabotage helped nurture the next phase beginning by late 1936.

When shortages were encountered, when unrealistic targets were missed, the tendency was to blame deliberate "wrecking." In light of the rhetoric of grandiose achievement, seemingly *only* the machinations of saboteurs, enemies, and wreckers could explain the anomalies and failures, the unexpected turmoil.

Periodic purging of the Communist Party was routine and should not to be confused with terror. But given the wider political dynamic in course, the purging process tended to spin out of control, producing unforeseen extremes. At some point, though experts disagree exactly when, purging of the party began snowballing into the Great Terror by late 1936, reached its peak in 1937–8, and concluded only in 1939. With the accent shifting from re-education to arrest, the 500,000 people purged from the party during 1937 were more likely than those previously to be shot or sent to the Gulag. The whole episode is often labeled the *Ezhovshchina*, after Nikolai Ezhov, head of the political police, called the People's Commissariat for Internal Affairs (NKVD) from 1934.

A reciprocal relationship between those above and those below was central to the overall dynamic. Responsible for the arrests and interrogations, the police almost had to proceed on their own initiative, to prove they were sufficiently vigilant, to avoid falling under suspicion themselves. Industrial workers proved more the agents of the Terror than its victims. Not feeling personally vulnerable, they tended to support Stalin's effort and eagerly denounced their "wrecking" superiors, sometimes even demanding that they be shot. The managers and other mid-level officials found themselves on a tightrope as they sought to survive scrutiny from above and below.

Much of this was not publicized, but there were also show trials intended for public consumption. The three Moscow trials of August 1936, January 1937, and March 1938 were particularly spectacular, especially the last, which brought the well-known communists Nicolai Bukharin, Alexei Rykov, and Genrikh Yagoda to the dock. Up to a point, at least, it was not irrational to believe that findings of guilt were justified, and the show trials fed the tendency to believe that systematic wrecking was going on. But whatever the grain of truth in each case, the situation became surreal, for not only were the accused confessing to crimes they had not committed, they were confessing to crimes that, for the most part, had not been committed at all.

Central though Stalin was to the Terror, the evidence indicates not coherent direction but confusion, indecision, mixed signals, and retreats throughout the process. Genuine fear and a sense that things were going too far appear to have mixed in his mind. With the Terror taking on a momentum of its own, the leadership had trouble checking it during 1938–9. In 1938, Ezhov, now himself a scapegoat, was ousted as police chief and arrested in an effort at restabilization, but executions proceeded at, if anything, a stepped-up pace under his successor beginning in November 1938.

It is by now widely agreed that terror in the Soviet case was not simply to atomize or manipulate, as for Hannah Arendt most famously. It stemmed from genuine fear, plausible up to a point but overblown because, caught up in the enthusiasm, the Soviets had come to believe their own propaganda, so that if there were problems, systematic sabotage must be going on.

By early 1939, the worst was over, but the death toll was high. Just how high remains controversial, but it was certainly in the hundreds of thousands. Overrepresented among the victims were senior party and government officials and especially industrial leaders. But the terror was not sufficiently widespread to have atomized society; for most, life went on. Many, especially among the young and idealistic, saw the Terror as justified and admired Stalin's toughness.

In any case, the Terror was an outcome, a by-product of the totalitarian mode of action. As such it was contingent, not necessary or essential, though it still may be considered a *likely* by-product in light of the difficult circumstances and the mode of action being attempted. The Terror left permanent scars and proved a breaking point in the evolution of the overall Soviet experiment. The bureaucracy, now insecure, grew cautious. More generally, the Terror scarred society, partly because it remained taboo. The Soviets could not come to terms with what had happened, and the original energizing idealism, based on the sense of creating a systematic alternative to liberal capitalism and fascism, diminished, eventually drying up altogether. Nationalism and a cult of Stalin came increasingly to set the tone. The key was not loss of belief in the nominal ideology but in the mode of action. Experience seemed to have shown that they could not act collectively as envisioned in a way that nurtured and sustained commitment and enthusiasm.

Differentiation and privilege proved incompatible over the long term with the energizing idealism that had initially sustained the experiment. Though everyone could contribute, grumbling about the privileges of certain workers and a wider resentment of privileged officialdom fed the tendency to excess and loss of control that then required a pulling back. The unforeseeable result was a combination of differentiation, hierarchy, and privilege, on the one hand, and resentment, cynicism, and passivity, on the other. This combination eventually yielded a certain kind of ossification.

The claim to be building socialism was largely a myth, but, as in fascist Italy, myth in the Soviet case was not merely manipulative, used by the leaders to extend their power over the others. Rather, it involved a cluster of images that, for a while, bound leaders and led together, fired genuine enthusiasm, and nurtured a capacity to tackle great tasks. But the surround of myth also contributed to the recklessness that made the great collective action ultimately self-defeating.

Nazi Germany

In Germany, more than in the other two countries, aspects of the prior situation especially seemed to warrant a totalitarian direction. The crisis of the Weimar Republic stemmed not only from the difficulties of multiparty parliamentary democracy but also from the tensions that arose as, under this new republic, the state expanded its reach in an effort to create a hypermodern welfare democracy. That had seemed necessary in light of all that war and defeat seemed to have revealed about Germany's long-term vulnerabilities. But the expansion of state functions proved somewhat chaotic, partly because of Germany's federal structure. Faith in the scope of social engineering gave way to a sense of impasse as the difficulties of acting from within a democratic framework came to light. But the necessary new action might be possible from within a post-democratic framework.

As an antidote to the Weimar crisis, *Gleichschaltung* – coordination of political institutions and procedures – followed immediately after Hitler came to power in January 1933. This reflected a further expanded reach for the German state, despite the Nazi emphasis on the *Volk* (people), movement, or Party. And the Nazi direction was overtly totalitarian, whatever the Nazis' hesitations about the term itself in light of its assumed link to Hegelian statism. That direction in Nazi Germany entailed not only a monopoly of political power and new modes of mass mobilization but also an expanded reach for the public sphere itself, requiring, most symptomatically, a new conception of law, an assault on the Christian churches, and a more interventionist population policy.

We have come to recognize the essential roles in the Nazi regime played by educated experts, whose participation cannot remotely be attributed to coercion. Many of them had concluded that Weimar democracy had remained too hesitant, with much discussion but too little policy deter- mination and action. To resolve the modern tensions that seemed to have come to the fore especially in Weimar Germany, it seemed necessary to combine technical efficiency with a more rigorous form of social control. Totalitarianism seemed the alternative to faltering, flabby democracy.[9]

Eugenicists like Fritz Lenz, co-author of an internationally respected 1923 treatise on heredity, turned to the Nazis as the only political party capable of translating eugenicist rhetoric into action. He was put off by Nazi anti-Semitism, but he lauded Hitler as early as 1930 as the first politician prepared to make "race hygiene" a serious element of state policy. Nazism proved the beneficiary of the Weimar crisis because it seemed uniquely capable of the new collective action required.

Certainly, Hitler was an ideologue of sorts. It is widely accepted that he operated on the basis of a worldview with four pillars: biological racism, anti-Semitism, social Darwinism, and geopolitics, which featured the geographical determination of power relationships among sovereign nations. Certain broad policy directions followed, from marginalizing Germany's Jews to the conquest of the living space (*Lebensraum*), putatively necessary for Germany to compete. But like Lenin and his heirs in Russia, Hitler sensed that a new mode of practice was necessary precisely because ideology could only carry so far. Extraordinary action was necessary – but it was also possible, it seemed, for those with the appropriate post-ideological insights into politics and history.

A sense of the requirements for a post-liberal politics informed Hitler's *Mein Kampf* (1925), where he discussed how will from above could interact with energies from below through new forms of mass mobilization and organization. And his idealism and commitment energized others, who were attracted not so much to some particular policy or ideological theme but to the more effective mode of collective action, transcending the divisions of bourgeois politics, which Hitler seemed first to promise, then to spearhead.

Sometimes Hitler seemed to suggest he was simply following laws of development or even serving "Providence." But the laws at issue were in fact no more helpful than those Lenin and Stalin claimed to derive from Marxism. Even while referring to such laws in *Mein Kampf*, Hitler expressed his sense of the fragility of things – but also the scope for giving order to the universe through will, strength, and organization. With his periodic references to "Providence," Hitler merely expressed his sense that the world is sufficiently coherent for history to be made to respond to human will – if the appropriate means were found.

Although, as we saw in the preceding chapter, some assume that the Nazis envisioned creating a sort of racial utopia, to be achieved once and for all, there was no scope simply to breed a master race, create a perfect society, and then relax. The unprecedented Nazi effort of population management could be experienced as grandiose, courageous, but it had to be ongoing, as part of the never-ending struggle to shape what the world becomes. More generally, the people's community (*Volksgemeinschaft*) that the Nazis sought to create would need constantly to be recreated, much like the totalitarian state in fascist Italy. And, for Germany, even success on the international level would breed a tendency to grow soft. Struggle with the Slavs concentrated east of the Urals would continue.

Like fascist Italy, Nazi Germany quickly embraced energetic action to tackle everything and anything, and the energy was contagious. The dynamic included a great deal of reciprocal interaction and initiative from below involving both Nazi Party members and ordinary Germans. Committed Nazis took the initiative by "working toward the Führer," an illuminating contemporary phrase indicating precisely the mutually reinforcing interaction of above and below. Hitler suggested a certain direction, and others did on their own what they assumed the Führer would want done, what the further development of the Nazi revolution seemed to require. But then such initiative from below often served both to pressure and to energize Hitler. Certainly, there were some genuine achievements, from building the Autobahns to pioneering the war on cancer. But even as he emphasized the scope for working toward the Führer, Ian Kershaw showed how it produced not only radicalization but also a chaotic loss of control.[10]

Totalitarian mobilization to create a *Volksgemeinshaft*, to forge a unified, enthusiastic nation capable of acting as one, was a central project. This was attempted most obviously through formal organizations like the Hitler Youth, the women's organizations (primarily the *Bund Deutscher Mädel*), and "Strength through Joy" (*Kraft durch Freude*), which organized leisure-time activities. These were vehicles of indoctrination that offered a sense of participation and enhanced the likelihood that ordinary Germans would get caught up in the Nazi project.

A variety of recent studies suggests that the Nazis engineered something like a moral and conceptual revolution, leading to a realignment of loyalties and a genuine experience of community. Internalizing the Nazi frame of mind, ordinary Germans came to identify with and participate in the regime's grandiose projects.[11] Whereas the earlier image of the Gestapo, or secret political police, terrorizing the population still lurks, research has shown that the vast majority had little reason to fear the Gestapo, which was underfunded and had to be selective in any case. In fact, the police effort to root out opponents or undesirables depended on the willingness of the wider citizenry to cooperate, to volunteer information, or to offer denunciations.[12]

The *Volksgemeinschaft* was to be based on racial homogeneity. Thus the achievement of community and belonging was bound up with the marginalization of those deemed outsiders. It was partly thus that anti-Semitism, while not central for most Germans at the outset of the Nazi regime, gradually became part of the consensus. Once the Nazis began singling out the Jews as the key obstacle to be overcome, other Germans, from leading eugenicists who had disliked racism to ordinary people who had not been especially anti-Semitic, acquiesced, grew indifferent to the fate of the Jews, even came to agree that Germany would be better off without them. These Germans were being drawn into an overall Nazi project that seemed to require homogenization and *thus* the exclusion of Jews. But common qualms and common complicity also cemented a sense of belonging and common participation.[13]

Nazi Jewish policy was part of a wider program of "race hygiene," a notion emerging before the Nazi period and combining the distinguishable strands of biological racism and eugenics. The premise was that society must take responsibility for shaping itself in a new, conscious way; only thus could it act effectively to shape history. And just as the Nazis assumed that they could not simply let nature take its course, neither could they leave the quality and quantity of the population to the aggregate of individual decisions, understood as private.

In the population sphere, especially, no private–public distinction was possible because the public implications of private decisions concerned the community's very capacity to act successfully. Yet all private decisions had public implications, so there could be no limit on either public intervention or individual responsibility. Thus the proclamation of labor-front chief Robert Ley that "the private citizen has ceased to exist."[14] Only sleep, said Ley, was private, and individuals were not free even to sleep whenever they wanted. Conversely, by implication everyone was participating all the time as they experienced the public weight of decisions earlier considered private.

Personal health, too, was central to the national interest. Individuals had no right to determine how to treat their own bodies – rather, they had an obligation to be healthy. And, as specified in a 1935 decree, the German medical profession had a duty to protect the health both of individuals and of the German people in the aggregate.

Whereas population engineering was common to all three regimes, it immediately became a central great task for Nazi Germany. The Weimar Republic had seen sporadic efforts in this direction, but the Nazis pointed beyond theory and advocacy to concerted action. Compulsory sterilization of those judged unfit to reproduce because of inheritable diseases and disabilities was introduced almost immediately, in 1933. The Nazis were following earlier examples, especially from the United States, but they were determined to do it more systematically and extensively. And such categories as "congenital feeble-mindedness," "manic depression," and "serious physical deformities" left broad discretion to those actually implementing the law. Through several follow-up measures, compulsory sterilization was extended to "the asocial," from criminals to vagrants to the "work-shy" – those who, for whatever reason, had "dropped out."

Though not the inevitable next step, the actual killing of those deemed unfit, beginning in 1939, surely found an important precedent in the forced sterilization campaign. But in commencing this so-called euthanasia program, there was no formal legislation or public discussion, and the regime made every effort to keep the operation secret. Still, widespread propaganda, especially through films, sought to build support for the overall direction. "Euthanasia," the regime suggested, could be legitimate, even a higher duty, restoring the natural order against the sinful human effort to preserve "life unworthy of life." By August 1941, when the official, centrally directed program was halted, more than 90,000 adults had been killed. But the killing of both adults and children continued in a more decentralized way thereafter.

Even the "euthanasia" program elicited a surprising degree of cooperation from ordinary Germans, who were apparently not averse to having the state kill sick relatives.[15] The Nazi atmosphere had altered the threshold of response – to some extent, at least, not by undermining morality but by redirecting it. In acquiescing in the deaths of family members, individuals might even have felt a sense of enhanced participation in offering personal sacrifice for the higher cause of national effectiveness.

It was a major radicalization actually to kill "life unworthy of life." And once the Nazis had done so, not only the precedent but the very availability of methods and personnel would affect, possibly decisively, the outcome of the parallel strand of Nazi population policy, revolving around racism and anti-Semitism.

The Holocaust, the systematic extermination of Jews and others, has come to seem the defining outcome of the Nazi experiment and even of totalitarianism more generally. But it must be understood not as some abiding goal but precisely as an outcome – an outcome of the project of radical population engineering. Hitler surely intended to find some "final solution" to Germany's "Jewish problem," but the term "final solution" was not a euphemism for extermination but a generality, suggesting definitive and complete. Despite Hitler's sometimes reckless rhetoric, and brutal though he and other Nazi leaders surely could be, the evidence is overwhelming that they did not decide to exterminate Jews as a matter of policy prior to 1941. And the magnitude and even character of the project changed even after it was decided to begin killing Jews. What is to be understood overall is neither an abiding intention nor a single event but a complex, layered process – "the twisted road to Auschwitz," as aptly charac-terized by Karl Schleunes in his pioneering book of that title, first published in 1970.[16]

At first, operating solely within Germany, the Nazis imposed restrictions and isolation on Jews in an effort to force them to emigrate. Key steps along the way were the Nuremberg laws of 1935, severely restricting the citizenship rights of German Jews, and the *Reichskristallnacht* (Crystal Night) pogrom of 1938, which saw the systematic burning of synagogues and the looting of Jewish-owned shops. Typical of totalitarian implementation, however, the effort to foster emigration was improvised, often incoherent, and mixed uneasily with other impulses, including the most banal greed.

Policy changed with the conquest of Poland in September 1939 and then again with the invasion of the Soviet Union in June 1941. It is crucial, as Christopher Browning has argued, that once the war had begun, "Nazi Jewish policy was part of a wider demographic project that aimed at a racial restructuring of eastern Europe... . Within this wider demographic project, Jewish policy did not *yet* have the priority or centrality in the Nazis' own sense of historical mission that has been argued for on the basis of what happened later."[17] The overall priority was German reset-tlement, reflecting the long-standing preoccupation with living space. The Nazi regime was to populate former Polish territories with ethnic Germans, thereby expanding spatially the ethnically homogenous community. To secure territory and cement the permanent subjugation of Poland, the Nazis set out, in a marked escalation of violence, to kill off the Polish elite, seeking to eliminate carriers of Polish national identity.

In September 1939, Poland had the largest concentration of Jews in Europe, about 3,250,000, or almost 10 percent of the population. Whatever was to happen to the bulk of the Polish population, the Jews, for the Nazis, constituted a distinguishable problem. But in this initial stage, focused on ethnic German resettlement, the Jews were merely a nuisance, their eventual fate secondary – and genuinely uncertain.

Polish Jews were initially confined to ghettos, subject to malnourishment and poor sanitation. Facing serious threats of disease, the ghettos themselves became a problem. The decisive steps toward the liquidation of the ghettos took place in interface with the Nazi assault on the Soviet Union that began in June 1941. In preparing for the invasion, Hitler made it clear to his top collaborators that this was to be an escalation, a war not only of territorial conquest but of race, ideology – and extermination. Within months, the Nazis had decided simply to kill the Jews they encountered rather than having to round them up later. This would head off the problems that ghettoization had produced in Poland.

But those problems continued to fester, prompting planning during the summer of 1941 for a complete solution to the Jewish question within all German-controlled territory. This was not merely a diktat from above. Pressure from below, from those in charge of the ghettos, responding to the worsening impasse the regime had created though its poorly coordinated action, had helped focus thinking at the top, speeding determination for a more radical course. In October 1941 the regime began constructing the first extermination camps, eventually numbering six, all in what had been Poland. Gassing experts from the "euthanasia" program were immediately involved.

Well into 1941, the Nazis had favored German Jews, most notably by prohibiting the emigration of non-German Jews to keep slots abroad open for Germans. But a series of measures in September and October 1941 specified that the 150,000 Jews remaining in Germany were to be deported to the east to share the fate of the Jews already in Poland. Only from this point did the Nazis seek to kill all the Jews within their grasp.

Even if it began helter-skelter, by 1942 the magnitude of the enterprise was clear – and itself energizing, at least for some. Thus the "extraordinary elation" that Saul Friedlander noted among the perpetrators.[18] The Nazis experienced their overall enterprise *not* as normal, routine – but as extraordinary, world-historical, even apocalyptic.

The decision to kill Jews emerged in steps, responding to circumstances not always foreseen. Even a coherent conception of how they would actually carry out mass extermination – special camps, factories, poison gas – emerged only gradually. But a totalitarian momentum was in progress. In light of the initiating aspiration and mode of action, it was no accident, once the Nazis had carried out sterilization and begun preparing for war, that they had embarked on "euthanasia," and thus it was no accident that the techniques and personnel were available or that the precedent was on the table, all feeding the particular extreme outcome: factory-like genocide.

The effort at totalitarian action in Nazi Germany produced a strange but characteristic combination by the end. During the course of the war, even some of those most energized by Hitler's seemingly limitless will came to perceive the flaws in the modes of decision making and organization that had developed during the course of the regime. By 1943, propaganda minister Joseph Goebbels recognized that the regime faced, of all things, a leadership crisis, as Hitler vacillated and neglected domestic issues. But there was little to be done. Possibilities had narrowed with the interaction of forces that had resulted from the new mode of action since 1933. The outcome was a fragmented regime of competing fiefdoms, unable to check Hitler, suffering from both choking bureaucracy and overall administrative chaos.

Hitler retained his faith that resolute will would somehow pay off in the end. The war effort could be renewed through radicalization on the home front, based on common austerity and sacrifice. But he increasingly lived in world of illusion, partly because of what his collaborators were telling him about new aircraft, wonder weapons, and the like. The overall Nazi stress on positive thinking, on the susceptibility of the world to willed action, was fatally compromising assessment of actual prospects.

From the earlier to the later cases

So we have a sense of what was totalitarian about the three earlier regimes, but we also better understand how elusive the category is. We were applying it to moving targets, to complex, uncertain trajectories, not to systems of rule or even to fixed, ideologically grounded programs. When we turn to later cases, we find that some are, if anything, still more complicated. In dealing with contemporary China, Iran, or Russia, there is no consensus on whether totalitarianism is applicable at all. Some authorities studiously avoid the concept; others use only a stereotypical version. As we approach those cases, we must first consider what seems to be going on, asking how the category might further understanding, not seek to assess those cases in light of criteria specified in advance. Because the cases and even particular episodes are often ambiguous, some formulations will be somewhat tentative or vague. But in each case we can come to an unambiguous conclusion based on explicit criteria of totalitarianism.

4
Movements and Regimes Since World War II

The waning of communism in the Soviet bloc

With the collapse and discredit of the two fascist regimes, it became much harder to take totalitarianism as the wave of the future. However, the communist experiment continued in the Soviet Union after 1945 and even spread to the new Soviet satellite states in east central Europe. After Stalin's death in 1953, there was some tempering of the totalitarian impulse under Nikita Khrushchev, who had emerged as his successor by 1956. However, though the most obviously totalitarian phase of the Soviet experiment was over, the Soviet regime was widely labeled totalitarian thereafter, as were the satellite states.

These included the German Democratic Republic (East Germany), Poland, Czechoslovakia, Hungary, Romania, and Bulgaria, with Yugoslavia and Albania sharing in communism, and arguably totalitarianism, but developing greater independence in their relationships with the Soviet Union. Even apart from these two relative outliers, the Soviet bloc was not monolithic, though a totalitarian direction was evident in each country.

These regimes were not merely foreign impositions, but an element of artificiality surrounded them from the start, and they proved subject to cynicism and decay. As I noted in chapter 2, the mechanisms were famously analyzed, while in progress, by Václav Havel and others. As the system was nearing the end, people simply went through the motions, performing rituals in which even the leaders no longer believed. Finally the whole Soviet system came apart during 1989–91 as the communist leaders essentially gave up power – a move that had seemed inconceivable in a totalitarian system.

The subsequent effort to build capitalist democracies on the ruins of the communist system proved complicated, though more so in some places than others. The enduring legacy of totalitarianism itself complicated the transition. I will consider the most important example, Russia, in the next chapter.

Beyond Europe: the Chinese communist experiment

Outside Europe, too, totalitarianism during the postwar period is most plausibly applied to regimes with some connection to Marxism or communism, for the most part in Asia. The most important is clearly the People's Republic of China, founded when the communists came to power in 1949.

In terms of the totalitarianism question, communist China has gone through three distinct phases. During the first, under Mao Zedong, China was surely totalitarian in intention and direction, but after his death in 1976, and especially with the reform beginning in 1978, his successors deliberately withdrew from what had come to seem the excesses of the Mao era. Now led by Deng Xioping, the system became less overtly totalitarian, though there were continuities as well, so the new phase bore a complex relationship with what had gone before. But innovations following the rise of Xi Jinping to the leadership by 2013 have seemed to some observers to constitute a return to totalitarianism – and thus a third phase.

The Chinese Communist Party was founded in 1921 as part of a wider reaction against what seemed the humiliating treatment of China by Japan and the western victors after World War I. To hold its own in the world, China seemed to require radical change, even if it meant following a western model. One possibility was Marxism-Leninism, just being tried out in practice for the first time in Russia. But though the Chinese, in embracing communism, fastened upon a foreign model, there was always a nationalistic edge to Chinese communism, partly because Marxism-Leninism had to be made relevant to China's special features but also because of Chinese resentment and pride.

The Chinese communists' struggle for power from 1921 to 1949 was far longer and more tortuous than the insurgent movements faced in Russia, Italy, and Germany. This period saw Japanese invasion in 1935, leading to ten years of war that became part of World War II. Uneasy cooperation between the communists and the dominant nationalist Guomindang (Kuomintang) marked the war years, but civil war followed, with the communists finally ousting the nationalists and achieving a monopoly of power on the Chinese mainland in 1949.

Central to the rise to power was the Long March of 1934–5, during which the communists endured great hardship at the hands of the advancing Kuomintang army. Thereafter, they would invoke the Long March in calling for renewed self-sacrifice and commitment to communist ideals. And it was the Long March that brought Mao to the leadership of the party.

After the march, the Chinese Communist Party established itself in Yan'an, a small provincial town that remained the party's headquarters until 1947. During the Yan'an period, the communists began building an alternative society, so that totalitarian programs and procedures were already in place when they finally achieved power on the national level in 1949. Two features are particularly worthy of note: thought reform and "the mass line."

Within the Marxist universe, Mao was on the idealist-humanist side of the spectrum. Thus, despite some premium on class background, he viewed "proletarian" less as an objective class than as an outlook, a set of values that could be learned by anyone through thought reform or "rectification," education into correct thinking.[1] Some would refer to "brainwashing," as used by Robert Jay Lifton in his *Thought Reform and the Psychology of Totalism: A Study of "Brainwashing" in China* (1961), which we discussed in chapter 2. Such thought reform was a priority for Mao even during the Yan'an period. Indeed, he laid down the principles of punishment and cure in a speech to party members in 1942, frequently quoted thereafter.

By then, programs in place were targeting two broad categories of people. First were captured enemies, especially opponents in the Chinese civil war, so that when the communists took power in 1949 they were prepared to deal with entire armies of prisoners. Second, they went after intellectuals, many of whom were sympathetic to the communists but who, with their urban lifestyles, seemed especially prone to "bourgeois" individualism, subjectivism, sentimentalism – especially prone to place their own interests above those of the people, as interpreted by the party.[2]

The thought-reform effort was not remotely a matter of atomizing the society or proving that anything is possible. Nor, as we noted in chapter 2, was the approach based on coercion, let alone torture. For Lifton, the key was the group dynamic fostering self-examination, shame, and confession. Those in the group competed to outdo each other in confessions. At the same time, those undergoing rectification learned noble goals of public service. This elicited some genuine enthusiasm, so it was not merely stifling individuality and spontaneity. Upon completion, most of those who had undergone the experience felt relief, but also a sense that they had bonded with the regime. Insofar as those in charge encountered resistance or foot-dragging, they imposed forced labor, but such repression was a by-product, not the underlying purpose.[3]

Although thought reform intertwined with other aspects of the communist program, Mao would turn to it periodically, obsessed as he was with ideological purity and the possibility of backsliding or revisionism. Up to a point, Lifton convinces even today with his somewhat ambiguous conclusion about the effectiveness of Mao's thought-reform effort. On the one hand, the repetition of the effort bred diminishing returns. The maximum effectiveness, Lifton suggested, was probably achieved early on, in 1951–2; thereafter, there was more coercion, less enthusiasm. But each wave made the next wave more necessary. Caught on a treadmill, the leaders could neither achieve perfection nor cease trying. They were the victims of their own cult of enthusiasm. But for Lifton that was only half the story. The leadership did manage to achieve a new ideological culture, even as the process produced resentment and diminished spontaneity at the same time.[4]

Nonetheless, the subsequent development of the Chinese experiment would defy Lifton's image of a treadmill. In fact, the experiment would spin out of control as intensification eventually led to the Cultural Revolution of 1966–76, which proved decisive to the fate of the first phase.

In addition to such thought-reform efforts, the communists early on stressed broad popular consultation and participation through "the mass line," a formula coined in 1928 but given classic formulation by Mao in 1943. The leadership was to take inchoate ideas from the masses, make them coherent, and in that form propagate them back to the masses. The masses would then embrace those ideas as their own and test them in action. In short, the leadership did not know what to do on its own; the mode of action required reciprocity, constant dialogue between leaders and led.[5]

Experts are generally willing to recognize that the communist effort to remake China yielded significant achievements during the early years, which saw much genuine enthusiasm and pride. Roderick MacFarquhar notes that from 1949 to 1956 Mao accomplished "the fastest, most extensive, and least damaging revolution carried out in any communist state." His most signal accomplishment was in pushing collectivization in agriculture far faster than other top leaders thought prudent.[6] The land reform of 1949–50 broke the power of the landlords. More generally, the new regime promoted public ownership of land, a reduced role for the family, and other measures to enhance social equality. There were rapid advances in literacy even as the education system became a vehicle for communist indoctrination.

In addition, the communists embarked on typically totalitarian population engineering, though in a relatively mild natalist form. Mao believed population to be China's key resource and exhorted his countrymen to have as many children as possible – as a communist duty.[7]

For most of the Mao period, the Chinese economy was almost entirely state run. And like the Soviets a generation before, the Chinese assigned priority to industrial development. Initially, they largely followed the Soviet model, with the first Five Year Plan for 1953–7 and the central procurement of agricultural production to finance investment in capital goods. More generally, the Chinese relied on Soviet financial support and technical assistance. Much as in the Soviet Union earlier, it all seemed to work to promote industrialization at first, though the countryside suffered.

Although his regime had achieved some successes by 1956, Mao tended to work by fits and starts, constantly worried about the flagging of revolutionary enthusiasm. Especially as the course of the Soviet Union under Nikita Khrushchev seemed to indicate revisionism, Mao abandoned the Soviet model in favor of a specifically Chinese alternative, "the Great Leap Forward" of 1958–60 – intended to reach socialism in one giant leap. Rural land, housing, and property were collectivized into vast, semi-autonomous communes, each with 5,000 families, and each with dormitories, cafeterias, and a common work plan. Each was even supposed to make its own steel in "backyard furnaces." The government took a large portion of the harvests to feed the cities. The experiment fueled a utopian fervor at first, but with bad weather, famine and mass starvation ensued. The famine of 1959–61 cost 20–30 million lives.

The Great Leap Forward is widely considered a disaster, and a retreat followed in the early 1960s. But then Mao, still obsessed with the danger of revisionism, launched an even more pervasive effort in 1966 with "the Great Proletarian Cultural Revolution," which continued for ten years until it was quickly wound down after his death in 1976. The regime bypassed or simply destroyed intermediate bureaucratic structures in an effort to reach the bottom of society to promote economic growth and egalitarianism. Universities were closed as students were sent to the countryside to learn from the peasants. There were mutual denunciations as Red Guard youth gangs terrorized communities. And now Mao became subject to mindless adulation as *The Little Red Book* of Mao quotations became ubiquitous. Timothy Cheek suggests that the

Cultural Revolution even outpaced Stalin's Russia as the closest realization of Orwellian dystopia.[8]

Certainly, the Cultural Revolution was the apotheosis of totalitarianism in communist China, but it was not about atomization, out-group hostility, redemptive violence, or even, at bottom, arbitrary arrest and confinement to cement power. But it did involve rekindling thought reform, which reached a new peak. The whole effort was intended above all to renew revolutionary enthusiasm, but it proved counterproductive in light of an unforeseen negative feedback mechanism, another instance of totalitarianism spinning out of control.

The mechanism was persuasively outlined by Susan Shirk in an influential article of 1984. She suggested that social systems can usefully be differentiated by occupational selection, and that Mao's China was a "virtuocracy," rewarding those with the desired ideological commitments. This was in contrast with both meritocracy, selection according to achievement or promise, and with feodocracy, selection according to characteristics like class, race, gender, religion, and native region. In China, virtuocracy seemed promising at first because revolution in the name of selflessness, of serving the people, had broad support.[9]

By the eve of the Cultural Revolution in 1966, Shirk pointed out, virtuocracy had produced distrust within particular organizations but not yet much alienation from the values of the revolution. The principles of selflessness were still revered, and it was considered proper for the party to shape people into this mold. Many, especially among the youth, were eager to participate in the crusade to defend the revolution against selfishness and competitiveness.[10] But with the Cultural Revolution, everyday life became a minefield of risks as people were subject to judgment by peers as well as by those higher up. All were expected to participate in the mutual surveillance and criticism.[11]

The basic problem, Shirk pointed out, was the vague and subjective standards for virtuocratic distribution. This made it easy to cheat up to a point, but the possibility of opportunism made people especially sensitive to the difference between sincerity and hypocrisy. People could see that it was not really virtue that was rewarded but the ability to ingratiate oneself. The outcome was opportunism, sycophancy, and patronage, on the one hand, and cynicism and alienation, from each other and from the regime, on the other. It became advisable to avoid activists within organizations, and people tended ultimately to turn inward, away from the public, political realm and into the private world of friendship and family.[12] This, of course, was precisely the opposite of the totalitarian intention, yet it is congruent with the self-defeating traits that have proven characteristic of totalitarianism in practice.

When Mao died in 1976, reaction was already building against the Cultural Revolution and, though a brief but bitter struggle followed his death, the outcome, clear by 1978, was a backtracking to reform of an entirely different sort. The far more pragmatic but still communist Deng Xiaoping spearheaded the change of direction. Although he was never party secretary, he was the regime's dominant figure from 1978 until his death in 1997. At a pivotal meeting in December 1978, the Central Committee of the Communist Party repudiated the Cultural Revolution and embraced Deng's policy of economic reform and modernization. Now the premium was to be on expertise and competence as opposed to ideological purity.

Even with the turn from Mao's policies, however, his legacy remained central to the legitimacy of the regime. The ideas, synthesized as "Mao Zedong thought," continued as the official ideology, as they are still today, though it is now emphasized that many besides Mao contributed. Portrayed as Sinified Marxism, "Mao Zedong thought" simply sums up the revolutionary experience of the party.[13] And it includes much reference to nationalism, the throwing off of imperialism, and the rise of China in the world under the communists.

Population engineering continued, though took a radically different direction in 1979. Couples were now limited to a single child in an effort to stem overpopulation in the world's most populous country. But most basically at issue were the political and economic spheres, interpenetrating but distinguishable.

Writing in 2015, Teresa Wright noted that "the totalitarian social and economic controls of the Mao era have

largely gone by the wayside, as has the continual incul-
cation of Maoist ideology."[14] But she also pointed out that
the actual structure of the political system was virtually
unchanged. China remained a one-party state, controlled
by the Communist Party, with power flowing from the top
down. Although the mass line continued, the public had
no say in choosing the leadership. Still, the selection of
top leaders was far more meritocratic and regularized than
under Mao, and those in charge were better educated, more
pragmatic, and less ideological.[15]

Economic growth became the highest priority, trumping
ideological orthodoxy. So whereas for most of the Mao
period the economy was almost entirely state run, after
Mao the communists took a pragmatic approach, constantly
experimenting, testing, and readjusting. State ownership of
most large enterprises and the banking system continued, but
gradually China opened to foreign trade and investment, and
private businesses were allowed to play a major role within
what remained a state-directed system.

By the early years of the twenty-first century, China had
developed a unique hybrid economy that was achieving the
highest rates of economic growth in world history, with gross
domestic product (GDP) increasing at an average of 9.63
percent a year from 1989 to 2018. During the first decade
of the century, China overtook Japan to become the world's
second-largest economy. By 2018, some were predicting that
China would overtake even the United States within a decade.

Meanwhile, the concern for consultation and reciprocity
continued, so policy decisions were always somewhat provisional, subject to revision according to the masses' responses.
Ordinary people were not, and did not feel, powerless.[16]
But though the government might sympathize with protest
against local abuses, for example, it would not tolerate
challenges to the overall system, including the monopoly of
the Communist Party.

The limits became dramatically clear with the bloody
crackdown on pro-democracy protesters in Tiananmen
Square in Beijing in 1989, as the communist regimes were
collapsing in Europe. More recently Liu Xiaobo, spearheading the Charter 08 protest of 2008, signed by 303
Chinese intellectuals and human rights activists, demanded

fundamental reform. He was awarded the Nobel Peace Prize but was locked up by the Chinese authorities. The West tended to support anyone challenging Communist Party rule, but such outside pressure fueled nationalism, arguably blunting any public demand for democratization.[17]

With regard to the totalitarianism question, the key is arguably the degree of pressure, or expectation, to participate. Writing in 2010, Timothy Cheek stressed the pulling back from totalitarianism, even the scope for opting out:

> While China is still an authoritarian state and not a democracy, no longer does the orthodoxy of the [Chinese Communist Party] dominate public discourse – writers and readers have the opportunity to explore alternate readings of Mao Zedong Thought, Marxism, or even liberalism, and more blessedly, all have the right at present to choose not to discuss political ideology at all.[18]

So whatever the limitations on democracy and freedom of expression, this was no longer totalitarianism. But even as China's rise to world power galvanized enthusiasm, by the first decade of the present century some in the leadership came to worry about a loss of ideological coherence, making revitalization necessary. The effort arguably entailed a return to totalitarianism, as we will see in the next chapter.

Radical Islam or "Islamism"

In the decades since 1945, totalitarianism has been applied not only to communist systems but also to radical Islamic movements and regimes. However, its use is more controversial for Islamic political ideas and practices, putatively based on religion, than for those based on communism, a political outgrowth of secular Marxism.

The most notable instances of the new Islamic extremism have been the Islamic Republic of Iran, founded with a 1979 revolution, and the Islamic State in Iraq and Syria (ISIS), established in 2013. But wider movements have also been implicated, such as the Muslim Brotherhood, which emerged in Egypt as early as the 1920s, Hamas in Palestine, Hezbollah in Lebanon, the Taliban in Afghanistan, and the Tehrik-i-Taliban Pakistan in Pakistan. Some of these movements have briefly held or shared power. Within this company, some have been more moderate, others more extreme, but the difference mostly concerns strategy and tactics as opposed to ideas and aims.

The nature of Islamist extremism is one of the most sensitive and contentious issues in modern history. Terrorism, especially, has undeniably provoked an Islamophobic backlash. But the excesses of that backlash say nothing about the nature of Islamic extremism. More than any one movement or regime, what first must be analyzed through the prism of totalitarianism is the overall ideology that the various Islamic political movements share to a considerable extent. Some call it "Islamism" to distinguish this overtly political orientation from Islam the religion, founded by the prophet Mohammed on the Arabian peninsula in 622.

Some such distinction is surely warranted, but it is important that Islam had an especially political and worldly side from the beginning, comprehensible in light of the hostility the new religion faced at the outset. To take root, the religion required a polity, a community of believers, under the leadership of Mohammed himself. Even the need for violence had to be considered. In short, there was less room for the sort of distinction between citizen and believer that can be found, for example, in Christianity.[19] But to grant that there is such a phenomenon as Islamism, distinguishable from Islam, is not in itself to say it is totalitarian.

After Mohammed's death, Muslims continued to be governed by a caliph, which simply means successor, essentially the prophet's steward on earth and the leader of the entire Muslim community. But the succession was contested upon Mohammed's death in 632. Through an extremely complicated sequence, the contest gradually produced the Sunni–Shia schism, which continues to divide Islam to this day. The Shia imams emerged as rivals or potential rivals to the Sunni caliphs.

Meanwhile, the caliphate endured under three different dynasties until it was ended by the Mongols in 1258. In 1517, the Ottoman Turks formed a new caliphate, which lasted until 1924, shortly after the breakup of the Ottoman

Empire as a result of World War I. The quest for another caliphate is central to the Sunni strand of contemporary Islamism. Indeed, the Islamic State in Iraq and Syria (ISIS) proclaimed precisely such a new caliphate in 2014 as it changed its name simply to the Islamic State (IS). As such, the caliphate claimed the allegiance of all Muslims, but it was unlikely to win over the Shia. Although it is estimated that 80 percent of the world's Muslims are Sunnis, a few countries, most notably Iran and Iraq, are majority Shia. And as Shia, the Islamic Republic of Iran would provide a rival to any new caliphate in the quest to unify the entire Muslim community.

Whatever the differences within the new Islamist political extremism, its various manifestations have been part of a broader current claiming purity and authentic Islamic tradition. In that sense, they are part of Salafism, which seeks return to the practices of the first three generations of Muslims. As we have noted, use of the totalitarian category in this case may seem wayward especially insofar as totalitarianism is taken as secular, not religious. But those critical of Islamic extremism often link it explicitly to totalitarianism or fascism ("Islamofascism"), applying the terms virtually interchangeably.[20] They point to Islamist intolerance and anti-Semitism, opposition to democracy, and violations of human rights. But particularly central – and controversial – have been sharia law and jihad, categories specific to Islam that I will address below.

In featuring parallels between Islamism and European totalitarianism, the Iranian-born scholar Mehdi Mozaffari concedes that Islamism is based on religion whereas the three earlier European regimes were secular. But he insists that "their common denominators – in their sense of historical crisis, their utopian aspirations, their forms of leadership, and their cult of violent action – are at least as substantial as their differences." And they share opposition to the present world order seemingly controlled by western imperialist powers, taken as promoting liberal democracy in their own interests. Mozaffari plausibly argues that totalitarian ideologies and regimes are always revisionist, seeking to replace the present world order with one of their own. He concludes that "Islamism is a religiously inspired ideology based on a totalitarian interpretation of Islam, whose ultimate objective is the conquest of the world by all means."[21]

However, other observers have been skeptical or at least cautionary about any such wider application of totalitarianism to Islamism. Tzvetan Todorov acknowledged common anti-individualism and violence in the name of a hegemonic ideology, but he found the differences more important than the similarities. The earlier totalitarians rejected religion and envisioned states as actors. Partly for that reason, the scale of the damage they caused was qualitatively greater.[22] Peter Baehr similarly stressed the novelty of modern Islamic terror and its differences from classic totalitarianism, citing in Islamism its attenuated territorial base, its obsession with the putatively hegemonic role of the United States, and its potential access to weapons of mass destruction.[23]

In terms of the relationship between contemporary political Islamism and the Islamic religious tradition, we find an instructive diversity of opinion among three leading authorities, all originally from the Islamic world though subsequently based in the West. Even those who see contemporary Islamic extremism as an ongoing danger do not necessarily see it as implicating all of Islam or suggest that Islam is particularly prone to extremism. In insisting on the distinction between Islamism and Islam, the Syrian-born political scientist Bassam Tibi, himself a devout Muslim, portrays radical Islam as a strictly modern political recasting, inventing notions not part of the tradition and perverting key categories like sharia and jihad.[24] However, Tibi sometimes seems to gloss over ambiguities as he insists on the distinction.

At the other extreme is the Egyptian-born political scientist Hamed Abdel-Samad, who comes closest to denying any distinction between Islam the religion and Islamism the violent, intolerant political ideology. "Islam's ancient totalitarian features," he insists, go all the way back to Mohammed himself.[25] Whereas religions generally – certainly Christianity – may tend to exclusivism or a claim to monopoly, Islam has been virtually from its inception particularly prone to intolerance, violence, and enmity toward Jews.

In the middle of the spectrum, and more typical, is Mozaffari, who finds the relationship between Islam and Islamism simply ambivalent. They were nourished by the same sources, but there are many varieties of Islam. At the same time, there could be no Islamism without Islam.[26]

Undeniably, Islamic civilization has known periods not only of relative tolerance but of active collaboration and cross-fertilization with Christians and Jews. Some take that as the norm, as what is authentic to Islamic tradition. It certainly characterized what is widely considered, by Muslims and non-Muslims alike, the Golden Age of Islamic civilization, roughly from the eighth to the fourteenth century. But equally undeniably there have also been periods of intolerance and conquest, and others take these as the norm for Islam, or at least as an indication of an abiding extremist potential. At the same time, it is widely accepted that some schools of Islam were more rigid, dogmatic, and exclusivist than others.

Whatever the potential in Islamic tradition, there is little doubt that specifically modern changes, comprising the putative evils of secular modernity and the perceived threats to Islamic civilization, have fueled the emergence of Islamism as a distinctive direction. Some point to resentments from a sense of having fallen behind, resentments that emerged as far back as Napoleon's conquest of Egypt, then part of the Ottoman Empire, in 1798–1801. The subsequent decline of the Ottoman Empire, its defeat in World War I, and the abolition of the Ottoman caliphate by the new secular-leaning Turkish regime in 1924 deeply affected some Muslims' sense of their place in the world.

As opposed to a caliphate at least nominally unifying the entire Muslim community, the Muslim world fell under the western system of sovereign nation-states, formalized with the Treaty of Westphalia ending the Thirty Years War in 1648, and extended arbitrarily, especially to certain Muslim lands of the Middle East, after World War I. In the contemporary Islamic world, some deeply resent this order of largely artificial nation-states, which seem to rest on weak foundations. Thus the image of a new caliphate, uniting all Muslims, is especially attractive.[27]

More generally, "modernity" itself, with its free speech, its often messy liberal democracy, its multiculturalism, its freedom of religion, its separation of church and state, its drive for gender equality, and its loosening of sexual strictures, is perceived as threatening the distinctiveness of Islamic civilization. From this perspective, it was especially reaction against the evils of secular modernity that yielded a new, arguably totalitarian mode of Islam. Precisely insofar as it is totalitarian, in other words, Islamism is a modern response to specifically modern challenges, not the return to tradition it might initially seem.

It is generally agreed that this specifically modern political Islam dates from the founding of the Muslim Brotherhood by the Egyptian intellectual Hassan al-Banna in 1928. He remained central to the intellectual lineage of Islamism until his death in 1949. But arguably more important was Sayyid Qutb, the key Muslim Brotherhood intellectual from 1951 until his death in 1966. Widely considered his heir as the most influential Islamist has been Yusuf al-Qaradawi, born in Egypt in 1926 but later based in Qatar. Even in his early nineties, he remained an especially effective television presence.

Distinctive though they are, these modern thinkers harken back to certain earlier figures, especially Ibn Taymiyyah (1263–1328), part of the Hanbali school of Islamic juris-prudence, founded in ninth century Baghdad by Ahmad ibn Hanbal (780–855). Insisting on a literal reading of the Quran and the prophet's statements, it proved the most extreme of the four main schools of Islamic jurisprudence and lies at the core of Islamist fundamentalism today.

Although Islamic tradition has provided inspiration and direction, it is well documented that the Muslim Brotherhood developed during the interwar period in interaction with European fascism – especially with Nazi Germany. Admiration for Hitler and Mussolini among Islamist leaders continued even in the immediate aftermath of World War II.[28] Although some overstate parallels based on a stereotypical conception of fascism, taken as the embodiment of violence and intolerance, the import of the interaction and certain similarities can hardly be denied. Most basically, on both sides we find a rejection of the western mainstream, as led by Britain, France, and the United States, and an insistence on the need for a new world order.

We also find anti-Semitism, which had played a part in Islamic tradition, as in Christian tradition, virtually from the start, this despite the fact that in Islam Jews are entitled to protection as "people of the book." It was partly anti-Semitism that made Nazism attractive to the fledgling Islamists in the first place. So Muslim anti-Semitism is not primarily a result of the recent Arab–Israeli conflict.

In any case, Islamism remained on the fringes as a radical protest movement for almost 50 years, as pan-Arab nationalism and anti-colonialism became ascendant after World War II. The Islamist movement clashed with Arab nationalists and other secular currents. Indeed, the Egyptian secret police assassinated Hassan al-Banna in 1949 during the reign of King Farouk. Revolution ousted Farouk in 1952, but the succeeding pan-Arab nationalist regime under Gamal Abdel Nasser was no friendlier to radical Islamism. President Nasser ordered the public hanging of Sayyid Qutb in 1966. For the Muslim Brotherhood, aiming to restore the caliphate, Nasser was a usurper.

But just a year later, in 1967, the Arabs, led by Egypt, suffered a humiliating defeat at the hands of Israel in the Six-Day War. At this point, many in the Arab world began to find a new course necessary, and the discourse of Islamism, especially the radical version of the recently executed Sayyid Qutb, quickly displaced Nasser's pan-Arab nationalism.

Modern Islamist ideology rests on essentially three pillars, each of which might be considered totalist in implication. Most basic is belief in the unique potential of Islam to redeem the modern world, thanks to its way of conceiving the place of religion. The lineage centering on Qutb claims to be returning to the basics of Islam in shifting from otherworldly practices like Sufi mysticism to a this-worldly orientation. Religion cannot be merely personal and private. Faith must be manifest in action to bring society in accord with God's plan.

As Albert Bergesen explains in introducing a selection of Qutb's writings, this imperative seemed to require rejecting modern secularism and democracy, which had resulted from a deviation from the uniquely coherent brand of monotheism found in Islam. At the same time, Qutb insisted that there must be a political community with authority relations governed by the Quran, not by democracy. Even a perfect secular democracy establishes another deity, the state, demanding obedience to its laws. Thus to be a good democratic citizen is to deny God. More generally, the modern mainstream has come to value material well-being at the expense of a sense of divine origin. Only the worldwide reestablishment of Islam can cure this modern pathology and yield world peace.[29]

Bassam Tibi acknowledges that all Islamists share such a vision of remaking the world, but he denies that the vision can be found in Islamic scripture. Nor did scripture specify some Islamic form of state or government.[30] But Qutb and others in the so-called Islamic revival relied less on traditional Islamic learning, as conveyed by clerics, than on their own interpretation of Islamic texts. In doing so, they took inspiration from the Protestant Reformation within Christianity.[31]

Beyond the notion of world redemption, two more specific notions – sharia law and jihad – are central to any consideration of the totalitarian potential of Islamism. Each was undeniably prominent in Islamic tradition, sharia as a code of proper conduct, including correct religious ritual, jihad as the duty to defend Islam. But there are questions about the connotations that earlier came to attach to each, and thus there is considerable disagreement over the extent to which the contemporary Islamist understanding involves a return to tradition as opposed to a modern recasting.

Sharia, taken as absolutely valid, specifies proper moral conduct, but how far does it extend? William Beeman stresses the traditionally delimited range of sharia law; for example, it mandated modest dress for both men and women but not that women be veiled. In the contemporary Islamic world, moreover, sharia is for the most part applied flexibly. However, it was always subject to interpretation, and interpretations often conflicted.[32] Such openness to interpretation would seem to allow for hard-line interpretations, pointing toward totalitarianism, as the imposition of sharia by the Taliban or IS has arguably entailed.

Tibi is especially forceful in seeking to specify the novelty of the modern recasting of sharia. At some points he concedes that modern sharia is not sheer invention, that whatever the minimal reference to sharia in the Quran, all issues were subject to regulation by sharia, and that sharia law did not recognize freedom of faith.[33] But he still insists that any notion of a sharia state is novel – and totalitarian in implication.

Rather than a uniform legal code, earlier sharia consisted largely of ad hoc judgments by Islamic jurists. Only with the emergence of Islamism were there, first, claims that divine Islamic law covered all areas and, second, demands that sharia law be written into national constitutions. And for Tibi it is precisely the forced compliance through codified law that makes the recent Islamist recasting of sharia totalitarian.[34]

The meaning of jihad, too, is very much disputed. Some see jihad as integral to Islam virtually from the beginning, in light of Islam's particular intolerance of other religions. It might be understood as the duty not merely to defend Islam but also to foster Islam – by violence if necessary. Sayyid Qutb's call for proactive jihad to create a universal Muslim community drew especially from Ibn Taymiyyah, who not only proclaimed jihad as the highest duty but envisioned it as a long-term proposition.[35] Others, however, insist that the Islamist understanding of jihad is strictly a modern adaptation, bogus in claiming continuity with long-standing tradition.

Arab Muslims first engaged in wars of jihad from the seventh century, with the proclaimed goal of expanding Islamic civilization everywhere. Aggressive wars continued periodically into the seventeenth century. Even as he seeks to defend Islamic tradition, Tibi acknowledges the Muslim belief that spreading the faith is not aggression but fulfilling a Quran commandment: we have sent you forth to all mankind. Violence was to be used only against those who resisted, but there could be no perpetual peace with non-Muslims.[36]

The Byzantine Empire, which had lasted for more than a thousand years, was brought down with the fall of Constantinople in 1453 by Islamic conquest. As Tibi emphasizes, this was by no means self-defense but military aggression preceded by other wars.[37] But such conquest by Islamic powers need not necessarily be construed as religious jihad. Mozaffari notes that the Ottoman Turks saw Islam as simply a religion and not a world vision that had to be realized. They made war to expand territory and enhance the glory of the Sultan, not to make the world Muslim. Yet Mozaffari goes on to play down the importance of the Ottoman experience for later Islamic self-understanding.[38]

Whatever the measure of violent jihad in Islamic tradition, it certainly can be argued that contemporary Islamist notions of jihad are novel and totalitarian in implication. It was especially the sense that Islamic civilization was under siege that led to calls for a new world order. And the vision of such an order changed the nature of jihad, first in the thinking of Hassan al-Banna. Now jihadism came to mean world revolution. Subsequently, Sayyid Qutb proclaimed jihad in quest of a new Islam-based world order to be the duty of all Muslims. So the aim was not simply to create a caliphate unifying the existing Muslim community but to restore Islam to predominance.[39]

This wide role for jihad seemed to mandate a change in strategy and tactics. Earlier jihad had entailed state-sponsored warfare by regular armies, with some limitations on conduct. Modern jihadism departs considerably in encompassing irregular warfare and terror by nonstate actors.[40] Moreover, a cult of martyrdom, bound up with the duty of jihad, understood as holy war, further distinguishes contemporary Islamist jihadism. Such glorification of death as political sacrifice had not been part of Islam, not even jihad to spread religion.[41]

Islamist terrorism was initially directed against other Muslims, seen as corrupt stooges for cooperation with the West.[42] A prominent example was the assassination in 1981 of Egyptian president Anwar Sadat by Muslim extremists, who had attained a go-ahead from a prominent cleric. But terror became a more widespread weapon of jihad as Islamism grew in strength.

Even insofar as sharia and jihad could become extreme earlier, it took the challenge of modernity, as perceived by the Islamists, to turn them in a totalitarian direction. Each specifies what the believer must do, so at issue is not merely orthodoxy, or right belief, but orthopraxy, the prescription and enforcement of proper conduct.

The Islamic Republic of Iran

The most sustained experiment with Islamism in practice has taken place in the Islamic Republic of Iran, still very much a player on the world stage. It emerged from a revolution that overthrew the secularizing monarchical regime of Shah Mohammed Reza Pahlavi in 1979. Mehdi Mozaffari, the Iranian-born political scientist, opposed first the Shah but then also the new Islamic republic, so was forced into exile. As he sees it, the new republic has all the characteristics of totalitarianism, though it is novel in being based on religious foundations. Indeed, he finds it the most elaborated form of Islamist totalitarianism to date.[43] In the same way, Bassam Tibi, citing Iran's "formal but meaningless" elections, finds the regime a new totalitarianism, not "Islamic democracy."[44] Hamed Abdel-Samad prefers "fascism" as the critical term, but he has much the same set of phenomena in mind as he contends that "Iran was the first Muslim state to make modern Islamic fascism its state doctrine."[45] As evidence, he cites the execution of critics, the total surveillance of the population, the oppression of women, and the aggressive anti-Semitism.

But other specialists unsympathetic to the regime suggest that even if Islamism as a wider movement has totalitarian implications, any such characterization is inappropriate for Iran. Assessment is difficult, however, because analysts tend to bring a delimited conception of totalitarianism to bear on the evidence. For example, such broadly democratic features as responsiveness to the public are taken as making Iran un-totalitarian even though, as we have seen, totalitarianism can encompass such features. One leading authority who explicitly uses the category to assess the Iranian regime seems to understand totalitarianism as merely an oppressive police state, when a more illuminating set of questions regarding totalitarianism in the Iranian case might be raised.[46]

Though a modernizing reformer, the Shah was increasingly autocratic and remote. By the mid-1970s, opposition to his regime was broadly based, reflecting not only concerns for Islam but also for democracy. Still, as revolution brewed, there was broad support for a specifically Islamic republic to replace the Shah's regime, partly because Iran's Shia religious establishment had been politically active periodically and enjoyed credibility as an independent political voice.[47] In addition, the charismatic Ayatollah Ruhollah Khomeini emerged as the revolution's undisputed leader. Already a noted Islamic scholar, he became politically prominent in demonstrations against the Shah in 1963–4. He viewed the Shah's reforms, some seeking to advance the position of women – especially by giving them the vote – as threatening to Islam. Improving the status of women had been a key aim in the Shah's overall program of westernization and economic development. Khomeini was forced into exile for fourteen years, spent mostly in Najaf, Iraq, one of the notable centers of Shia learning. There, during the early 1970s, he produced a book, *Islamic Government*, proposing a form of direct clerical rule under the doctrine of Velayat-e Faqih, the regency of the jurisprudent, or supreme leader, who acts on behalf of the last of the early imams. Beyond the role of the supreme leader, Khomeini's book was thin on the details of governance; everything would be simple, with clerical rule based on Islamic law.[48]

Shia spiritual leaders had traditionally eschewed temporal power; clerical rule would invite corruption, endangering the purity of the faith. So most advocated secular rule, with the clergy limited to offering advice.[49] Khomenei's proposal for Islamic government immediately met opposition in Najaf from the powerful Ayatollah Abol-Qasem Khoei, who took a more traditional, quietist position, resisting direct involvement in politics. Even long after Khomeini's death in 1989, many Shia Muslim scholars see his views as heretical.[50]

After fourteen years in exile, Khomeini returned dramatically to Iran in February 1979, as the revolution was reaching its climax. But though it was a foregone conclusion that he would be the supreme leader in a new Islamic regime, dissent remained even among Iranian clerics about the model of governance that Khomeini had proposed. At the same time, the clerics remained well aware that, whereas there was broad support for a specifically Islamic regime, the revolution had had a genuinely democratic component, and they were not seeking a monopoly of power, which, they felt, would have been neither legitimate nor effective. So the new constitution merged religious and democratic elements, resulting in a hybrid of sorts, a state structure with interlocking leadership positions and numerous checks and balances. William Beeman has nicely labeled it "a miracle of complexity."[51]

Michael Axworthy, in an especially judicious account, concludes that Iran is not a functioning democracy, despite regular and mostly free elections and the willingness of losers to accept losses.[52] The power of the democratic side of government vis-à-vis the clerical side has remained limited in important respects. In the presidential elections of 1997, 2005, and 2013, Iranian voters managed to change the regime's direction to some extent, but there were strict limits to the change they could bring about in light of the power of conservative clerics.[53]

During its first few years, the regime took significant steps that indeed suggested a totalitarian direction, even to portend a totalitarian regime. The revolutionary situation itself had seemed to demand extreme measures, such as hostage-taking and terrorism against civilians.[54] Once power was won in 1979, it seemed imperative to consolidate the revolutionary regime against opponents and to ward off foreign interference, a genuine danger. Indeed, war with Iraq ensued almost immediately in 1980, lasting until a ceasefire in 1988.

Dominating events beginning in 1980–3 was the "Cultural Revolution," loosely under the Revolutionary Guard, which attacked and occasionally murdered people deemed a threat to the new regime. The Cultural Revolution temporarily closed the universities so they could be purged and "Islamicized." Half the academic staff was removed. There were also hundreds of executions for political dissent but also for narcotics or sexual offenses. Revolutionary courts replaced the previous civil codes with a particularly harsh version of sharia law. Several hundred judicial killings targeted especially functionaries of the Shah's regime.[55]

But things began to ease up by the end of 1982. There were steps to rein in the revolutionary courts and to follow regular judicial procedures, partly to reassure the middle class and to lure émigrés to return. So some of the most extreme of the earlier steps proved temporary. But the regime continued to zigzag, making for a certain ambiguity overall. During 1988–9, for example, the leadership lifted restrictions on political activity while also executing what seemed to be the remaining potential opposition leaders. Violence, repression, forced compliance, and government interference with the media returned periodically after the Cultural Revolution.

Exporting the revolution might constitute a mobilizing totalitarian great task, and it was surely on the agenda at first. Even the new constitution proclaimed the duty to export the superior Islamic Republic to the rest of the Muslim world.[56] At the outset, leading radical clerics strongly supported Khomeini's desire to export the revolution. One of the most influential, Ayatollah Hossein Ali Montazeri, referred to suicide bombing attacks in Kuwait in 1983 as acts "in performance of Islamic duty."[57] But experts disagree over how central exporting the revolution has remained to the regime's agenda. It is striking that, though suicide attacks were encouraged at first, they were subsequently outlawed by Iranian clerics even as they continued in Sunni Islam.[58]

Certainly Iran, as a large regional player, has remained active in power struggles in the Islamic world, and its rivalry with Sunni Saudi Arabia has become particularly bitter in recent years. But how much Iranian foreign policy is simply the normal pursuit of national interests, and how much it entails a totalitarian ideological project, is not clear. Iran has encountered special temptations but also special limits as the major Shia power in a region with Sunni states more powerful in the aggregate. In the early days, when Khomeini hoped to export the revolution and establish Iranian leadership, he played down the Shia–Sunni schism. But that abiding schism proved to limit Iran's reach nevertheless. In 2013, Axworthy unequivocally concluded that Iran was not seeking to export the revolution.[59]

Anoushiravan Ehteshami, writing in 2017, was more nuanced as he sought to make sense of what he took to be a somewhat vacillating, and sometimes mystifying, Iranian stance in foreign affairs. Iranian policy and practice, he convincingly argued, have been driven by both revolutionary idealism and pragmatic realism – and there was obviously a tension between them.[60] But that combination of idealism and pragmatism characterized the earlier totalitarian regimes as well.

However, as Shia, Iran has faced special obstacles, and Ehteshami accents the weakness of Iran's regional position, despite the country's pretensions and aspirations. The more Iran has tried to defend its Shia allies in Syria and Iraq and the Shia communities in Yemen, Pakistan, Afghanistan, and elsewhere, the more other states and Sunni jihadists characterize its behavior as sectarian, meddling, and hegemonic. To non-Shia Muslims, Iran appears as the aggressor, not as the Muslim world's just power and liberator. If anything, Ehteshami concludes, Iran's clout in the region has diminished since the advent of the Arab Spring in 2011.[61] So whereas exporting the revolution was arguably part of the regime's initial proto-totalitarian direction, the subsequent fate of Iranian foreign policy has manifested the limits of its totalitarian reach, even a turning away from the totalitarian effort.

But whatever Iran's prospects for leadership in the Islamic world, factionalism and disagreement about priorities have compromised any totalitarian will. This may seem surprising, given the common commitment to Islam and the appearance of unity under a supreme leader. But Ehteshami stresses that within a year of the regime's birth, the vagueness that had made possible the revolutionary coalition was no longer sufficient, and the coalition came apart. Since then, the largely clerical inner circle has been unable to create an acceptable vision or blueprint for the Islamic republic. As president from 1989 to 1997, Ali Akbar Hashemi Rafsanjani made a concerted effort to reform the economy but encountered a conservative backlash. That episode epitomized the process that has led to division into conservative and reformist blocs, representing starkly different visions of Iran and its place in the international system.[62]

We note such division even in areas that initially seem to suggest a unified sense of purpose. For example, partisans of the new revolutionary regime shared a fierce concern to remain free from outside interference of the sort Iran had experienced earlier, especially from Britain and the United States. But there have been strong disagreements over the implications of any western influence. When President Hassan Rouhani, trumpeting the nuclear agreement of 2015, predicted that it would open Iran to western investment, conservatives complained that this would also mean opening Iran to western social corruption.[63]

More generally, Axworthy noted that those in the ruling clique still wanted to believe they were democratic, but they feared that if freedom and democracy were given free rein, the Islamic revolution would be swept away in a flood of western cultural influence. He added that they were right to be worried because the regime was indeed vulnerable but also because, he noted explicitly, there were plausible reasons to dislike aspects of the western model.[64]

Certainly, the new regime has been concerned to protect the interests of Islam and to promote Islamic law, but even this sense of common purpose only carries so far. Although Islam is a religion, it allows for considerable flexibility, as we saw in considering sharia. So concern for Islam did not require dictating all aspects of life or heavy surveillance to ensure compliance. Conversely, Ehteshami noted that Khomeini's accent on the simple "Islamicity" of the regime was not sufficient to determine specific policies regarding the sociocultural realm, the economy, or foreign affairs.[65] So not only does Islam itself not inherently entail a totalist demand, it often does not indicate clear directives for policy.

In the secular realm, the revolution merged radical and conservative ideas, and the radical push came not just from secular activists who had opposed the Shah but also from clerics with progressive social aims. Disagreement over priorities quickly produced factionalism even among the clerics. A determination to improve the lot of the lower classes led to real improvements in such areas as health care and education. Primary education was extended to all, including girls. Improving living standards was a priority, and the regime made considerable progress under difficult circumstances. But whereas there was a social safety net, there was also great inequality in income, and conservatives were especially concerned to protect private property and promote free enterprise.[66]

Iranian courts had been controlled by the clergy until the early twentieth century, when they were secularized under the new Pahlavi dynasty. As we have seen, sharia law was then reimposed at the outset of the new revolutionary regime in 1979. We have also seen, however, that in Islamic tradition the scope of sharia is open to varying, often conflicting, interpretations. In Iran, the results of sharia have been mixed, indicating the limits of any totalitarian thrust.

On the one hand, hardline conservative judges have not only used the judicial system to undermine reforms but also, in the process, to close reformist newspapers and sometimes to imprison or even execute reformers or journalists. On the other hand, many punishments specified in Islamic texts, like stoning for adultery, have been eased.[67]

With the reimposition of sharia law early in 1979, the treatment of women became more restrictive than a mere return to Iranian tradition would have warranted. Male dominance was the rule so that, for example, women needed the permission of a husband or father to travel. Women lost custody rights in the event of divorce. However, these measures were met with peaceful protests, and the regime did not go as far as it might have in restricting the role of women – repealing the right to vote, for example.[68] And the status of women improved over the longer term as, for example, they became prominent in education and other significant areas of the workforce. But they remained subject to limitations on religious grounds. For example, they could not become judges or run for president, and their inheritance was only half that of male siblings.[69]

As we noted in chapter 1, totalitarianism entails exploitation of the education system. We have already discussed the purge of Iranian universities during the cultural revolution of the early 1980s, and during its first ten years the Iranian regime devoted much effort to ensuring ideological correctness in education. But under Rafsanjani's presidency from 1989 to 1997, there was less emphasis on religion or ideology and more on quality, to make education more useful. Rafsanjani even supported new private universities, an aspect of a wider turn from the statist ideological order of the 1980s. That turn was then the basis for reforms carried out under President Mohammed Khatami after 1997.[70] The reform effort encountered limits but, as in China, the turn from statism was a retreat from totalitarianism.

What about the treatment of minorities, and especially religious minorities, in a self-proclaimed Islamic state? We have seen that anti-Semitism had periodically been found in the Islamic world well before the advent of Zionism and the creation of Israel. Axworthy suggests that an unspoken bargain crystalized after the revolution: as long as Iranian Jews condemned Zionism and thus Israel, they would be left in peace to run businesses and worship in synagogues. Still, both Jews and Christians have suffered steady, low-level intimidation by the regime, with occasional flare-ups of greater nastiness. Many Jews have emigrated. The far larger Baha'i population has been persecuted more severely, but they are considered apostates from Islam, not adherents of an alternative religion that might be tolerated.[71]

In principle, the clerical oligarchy can always intervene to get its way, and sometimes it does, but sometimes it does not. This ambiguity obviously reflects a combination of factors in undecidable proportion – disunity among the leaders, a sense of vulnerability, some measure of democratic commitment, or at least recognition that the regime rests on a combination of democracy and clerical rule. And even within the clerical leadership, there have always been reformers, as we have seen. The result has been more back and forth than the consistent and even radicalizing hard line that would suggest a totalitarian direction.

The limits were evident most dramatically in the 2009 and 2013 presidential elections. In 2009, the relatively hardline but erratic Mahmoud Ahmadinejad was seeking re-election as president. Though disillusioned with him, the regime's clerical leaders interfered to assure his re-election against the more moderate, reformist candidate, thereby sparking months of protests. This "Green Movement" was the most serious challenge the regime had faced, and it prompted a violent response. Ayatollah Montazeri, once the likely successor to Khomeini but now a strong critic of the regime's authoritarian tendencies, was important to the protests and died under house arrest in December 2009. But the regime proved reluctant to use its full force against the opposition. Some leaders of the protest remained at large, still speaking out. And then in 2013 clerical leaders and the Revolutionary Guard accepted the election of Hassan Rouhani as president, even though they had favored more conservative candidates.

Among authorities who deny that the Islamic Republic can be considered totalitarian or fascist, Michael Axworthy is more willing than most to compare Iran with earlier cases, and such comparisons certainly serve evaluation. At one point, for example, he suggests parallels with the syndrome Václav Havel pinpointed in diagnosing the decay of communism in Czechoslovakia.[72] In Iran, too, Axworthy implied, the totalitarian potential seemed to be dissipating.

Two other of Axworthy's observations are still more suggestive. Even at the point where he equates a mere police state with totalitarianism, he offers an illuminating suggestion: "The stolen election of June 2009," he says, "may have taken Iranians closer to totalitarianism, but they are still not there yet." And he stressed how difficult it would be to maintain a police state in Iran. If the leadership squeezes politics in one area, it bulges out irrepressibly in another.[73]

In what might be taken as an example of what Axworthy had in mind, Ehteshami suggests that the factional struggles yield a complex play of forces with outcomes impossible to foresee. Reformist success in nuclear negotiations could lead to tighter controls at home by requiring women to wear the hijab and avoid cosmetics, by restricting clothing and hairstyles, by limiting the use of social media for youth, or by turning up the heat on intellectuals.[74] The two authorities spin the point differently, however, because for Axworthy the syndrome indicates a vitality that limits the scope for a police state, while for Ehteshami it is symptomatic of debilitating factionalism. But spun either way, we find a syndrome that delimits the scope for totalitarianism.

Axworthy also notes that whereas the majority of Iranians accept the regime's Islamic credentials, Islam is not susceptible to control by a regime – as Jacobinism was during the French Revolution and Marxism was in the Soviet Union. The comparison is undeveloped and might seem only to carry so far, but the bottom-line point that Islam is an independent standard, ultimately beyond the reach of the regime, is convincing and important. Axworthy goes further to suggest that whatever the ruling clerics themselves claim, if a critical mass of the public decides the regime has become un-Islamic, it will disappear.[75]

William Beeman goes further still in arguing that the regency of the supreme leader is not presently supported by theologians or the public.[76] The suspicion that surrounded direct clerical rule at the outset remains. And we must add that such suspicion is found not only among secularists but also among committed Muslims concerned that worldly politics is likely to prove corrupting to religion – and has indeed corrupted Islam in Iran. This sense breeds active hostility not only in the name of democracy but also in the name of Islam. The fact that earlier so much of the Shiite clergy in Iraq did not buy into Khomeini's model meant, and still means, that there remained an alternative source of direction and loyalty even within Shia Islam.

So what we find is not simply a tension between democracy and clerical rule or even – a step further – a democratic check on clerical rule and the totalitarian potential of religion. Whereas Islam in the Iranian case has fed the totalitarian impulse in certain respects, the religion was not monolithic and has itself constituted a check, a limit. The Islamic Republic of Iran is certainly an instance of Islamism, but it also suggests that, whatever the ideology and rhetoric, Islamism in power may fall short of totalitarianism.

However, the category certainly helps us understand the Iranian case, even indicating why its totalitarian potential seems largely to have dissipated. The same is true of China during the decades after Mao, even as it remained a repressive one-party system. But that is not the end of the story. What can we say about the future of totalitarianism?

5

The Future of Totalitarianism

In considering the future of totalitarianism, we must treat, on the one hand, aspirations, tendencies, and actions that might be labeled totalitarian and, on the other, the concept itself, especially in light of the skepticism that continues to surround it. Pondering the future of the concept requires asking how we might learn more deeply from the earlier instances – partly by recasting the totalitarianism category. Such deeper learning can serve our aim of preventing, or at least minimizing the scope for, renewed instances of totalitarianism.

Neo-fascism and populism

Movements and phenomena that seem to recall earlier fascism, whether or not they themselves claimed a link, have emerged in the western world ever since the defeat of the fascist powers in World War II. Roger Griffin has long insisted that fascism, reflecting a longing for palingenetic renewal, returned in new forms after 1945 – and continues today. He also notably denies that these new forms were totalitarian but, as he sees it, that does not make them any less fascist. Classic fascism, he argues, became totalitarian only because of the contingencies of "an age shaped by World

War I, the collapse of absolutist empires and the Russian Revolution of 1917," and its historically specific totalitarian form ended in 1945.[1] So we should not assume that totalitarianism is a defining feature of fascism.

But if there are aspirations, grouplets, and movements legitimately labeled fascist, is the lack of a totalitarian impulse simply from weakness? Conversely, would these entities become totalitarian if they managed to come to power? We cannot say, but, though there are common gurus like the French thinker Alain de Benoist, the groups that Griffin features remain weak and dispersed on the political fringes. Of more immediate concern has been the populist turn from within the democratic political mainstream in Europe and beyond. This has involved the emergence and growth of significant right-wing political movements with tendencies – authoritarianism, charismatic leadership, nationalist resistance to globalization and European integration, and xenophobic hostility to outsiders – that for many recall earlier fascism or totalitarianism. Slavoj Žižek included the new right populism in indicating the focus of fears of renewed totalitarianism.[2]

Nonetheless, the populist turn is not in itself totalitarian in implication. The totalitarian dimension of the earlier fascist regimes encompassed far more than xenophobia and the like. Griffin vehemently denies that contemporary right-wing populist movements in Europe are fascist, let alone totalitarian, because they continue to hold to democratic procedures.[3] But that hold may be tenuous, especially in countries of the former Soviet bloc like Hungary and Poland still seeking to work beyond the communist system, with its totalitarian tendencies. Though Viktor Orbán's Hungary displays undoubted authoritarian inclinations, it is not totalitarian in the earlier sense of vital experiment, of trying something new in response to a sense of novel challenge and opportunity requiring new modes of mobilization. Rather, the response has been more purely defensive. Indeed, Orbán likes to portray himself as the savior of the European Union, which he views as unsustainable in its present form.

Vladimir Putin's Russia

The most significant case is surely Russia itself, which turned haltingly toward democracy during the 1990s but which has gone in a different direction under Vladimir Putin since 2000. Russia's new constitution of 1993 gave considerable power to the presidency, but Putin has expanded that power at the expense of countervailing structures in the political system. With the neutering of the formal checks and balances, his has become, in Brian Taylor's words, "an authoritarian regime within the formal shell of democracy – what political scientists call electoral authoritarianism."[4] There is some scope for political opposition, though it is kept within strict limits. And there are elections, but Putin's ruling party cannot lose. Limited though they are, the democratic procedures in Iran are surely more substantial. In addition, Putin has limited human rights by extending control over the media, for example, and by cracking down on gays and lesbians.

However, it takes more than a "strong man" ruling with no effective term limits or opposition, to constitute totalitarianism. So, remembering that we need not insist on either/or, do we find totalitarian directions or at least potential in Putin's Russia? Do we find mass mobilization for great collective tasks or efforts to shape a "new man"?

Although Putin's background was with the Russian security apparatus, it does not appear inevitable that he would turn from democracy and become antagonistic toward the West. He seemed willing to cooperate at first, most notably in response to the 2001 terrorist attack on the United States. But then, beginning in 2003, he became increasingly disillusioned, first as the US invasion of Iraq in 2003 indicated US unilateralism. This was the first in a series of events that seemed to Putin and many other Russians evidence of western disrespect for Russia. They eventually came to feel that the West, and especially the United States, was seeking to weaken and isolate Russia, even to force it to break up in order to gain control over its considerable natural resources.[5] Underlying this quick-tempered response was the deeper feeling of humiliation that had accompanied the disintegration of the Soviet Union, ending its status as one of the two global superpowers.

An ongoing provocation was the expansion, or threatened expansion, of the North Atlantic Treaty Organization (NATO), even to include states such as Georgia and Ukraine that had not been satellite states but integral parts of the pre-Soviet Russian Empire. Putin complained that this directly threatened Russian security.

In 2008, border issues boiled over in two provinces of Georgia, each home to substantial numbers of Russians aspiring to break away. When the Georgian government attempted to reassert control, Russia invaded, easily defeating the Georgian army and consolidating Russian control over the two territories. Most western observers reacted with dismay at what seemed a resurgence of Russian imperialism. Yet some agreed with Russia that the West was hypocritically applying a double standard in condemning Russia for defending the right of the two provinces to secede from Georgia. Earlier that same year, they had recognized Kosovo when it unilaterally declared its independence from Serbia, against the wishes of Russia, Serbia's long-time protector.

At least as threatening to Russia as NATO expansion was the wave of "color revolutions," in which masses of ordinary people took to the streets to oppose autocratic regimes or protest electoral fraud. The West tended to support such opposition movements, and Putin and his allies saw the United States as behind them. A major example was the "Orange Revolution" of 2004–5 in Ukraine, which led to the defeat of the Russian-supported candidate in a disputed presidential election. These popular revolutions seemed so threatening to Putin because his own regime might be vulnerable. Seeming irregularities in the Russian parliamentary elections of December 2011 prompted serious protests, blamed on outside forces. The outcome was an embargo on perceived western values, including tolerance of homosexuality.

Ukraine remained a key sticking point, especially as the country seemed to turn away from Russia and toward the European Union and the West. In March 2014, Russia violated Ukraine's territorial sovereignty by seizing the Crimean Peninsula in the Black Sea. Prior to 1954, Crimea had been part of the Russian Republic, but it was then transferred to the Ukrainian Republic, still an integral part of the Soviet Union. It remained the home of Russia's Black Sea naval fleet even after Ukraine became independent. Russia's military takeover of Crimea was the first instance since World War II in which a sovereign European state had annexed the territory of another. Meanwhile, also in 2014, Putin provided military support for pro-Russian separatists in southeastern Ukraine, on the border with Russia, resulting in full-scale war with the Ukrainian government for some months and low-level fighting thereafter.

Among Russians, the annexation of Crimea propelled Putin's percentile approval ratings into the eighties, where they remained for several years. The West, finding Russia guilty of naked aggression in Ukraine, imposed sanctions in response. But Putin continued to go his own way, demonstrating Russian muscle. In September 2015, Russia intervened in the Syrian civil war in support of Bashar al-Assad's dictatorial regime, turning the tide in Assad's favor by 2019.

Meanwhile, Russia was engaged in cyber intervention in Europe and, most famously, in the 2016 presidential election in the United States through computer hacking and disinformation. But in Russia, as in China, the leadership viewed cyber not only as an opportunity but as a threat – especially as their populations seemed susceptible to wider propaganda and disinformation from antagonists abroad. Alexander Klimburg notes that Russia sees itself under attack as material over which the government has no control comes in through the internet, seeking, as Russia sees it, to undermine Russian sovereignty and territorial integrity.[6]

Whereas the United States, especially, clings to the present multi-stakeholder free internet, which is largely US-based but not government controlled, Russia and China call for the internet to be governed by the United Nations or some other supranational body – or better yet, for every country to have sovereignty over its own portion of the internet. Because the institutions are indeed US-based, it is not surprising that Russia and China charge that the United States insists on the free internet model because it serves US interests. And Klimburg grants that cyber-sovereignty proponents, led by Russia, have shown hypocrisies in the free internet argument.[7]

All these perceived slights and Russia's counterpunches do not in themselves suggest totalitarianism – but perhaps a totalitarian direction or potential? Even if it was not what fueled Putin's regime in the first place, do we find some wider, perhaps mobilizing, ideology or purpose surrounding these Russian responses?

Especially in light of Russian resentment of the West, Putin came under the influence of ideologues like the flamboyant Alexander Dugin, who has been referred to as "Putin's brain" and who has been influential in right-wing thinking across Europe. For Gerard Toal, Dugin is the most notorious of Russia's revisionist geopolitical thinkers, having, for example, denounced the independence of Ukraine in 1997, insisting that it made no geopolitical sense.[8] Notorious or not, Dugin had considerable success with *The Foundations of Geopolitics: Russia's Geopolitical Future*, published in several editions. Intended as a handbook for the Academy of the General Staff of the Russian Armed Forces, it includes an agenda for revisionist geopolitics across Eurasia.[9]

Dugin claimed to offer "the fourth political theory," necessary once the limits of liberalism, communism, and fascism had been shown up in practice. The three were not to be rejected totally; each offered valuable ideas that had remained on the periphery or been diluted or corrupted. Most basically, Nazism and fascism stood for community as opposed to liberal individualism as the be all and end all. But racism compromised their communitarian insight. The fourth theory, Dugin insists, rejects all forms of racism. Dugin also stresses the ongoing value of the Marxist critique of bourgeois capitalism. But, in the last analysis, both communism and fascism suffered from totalitarian excesses that had to be avoided.[10]

In the contemporary world, as Dugin sees it, liberalism is at once totalitarian and racist in insisting on its own universality, in insisting that one size fits all, in its intolerance of differences. Unipolar globalization imposes a local value as universal: "Globalization is thus nothing more than a globally deployed model of western European, or, rather, Anglo-Saxon ethnocentrism, which is the purest form of racist ideology." There is no objective basis for claiming that one society is superior to another.[11]

As an alternative, Dugin fastens upon "Eurasianism" in a way recalling earlier geopolitical theories that influenced Hitler's expansionism. Dugin sees a clash between land-based Eurasia, ideally to be led by Russia, and the maritime or Atlantic world, led by the United States. Whereas the land-based states prize history and tradition, the Atlanticist states prize individual freedom, which dissolves tradition and the bonds of community.

Putin's Russia is the natural leader in the resurgence of Eurasia, encircled by western liberalism. Russia is to lead and organize the Eurasian land mass, but Dugin cautions that no one nation can be the historical subject. Others can help Russia; conversely, Russia, in line with the emphasis on tradition, must recognize considerable autonomy for others.[12]

Up to a point, Dugin's vision is merely conservative and organicist and not in itself totalitarian, but it could serve totalitarian mobilization for collective action. And some feel that it has already, at least to some extent, in Putin's Russia. It provides a rationale and an imperative for expanding territorially at the expense of neighbors like Ukraine. And Putin's campaign against gays and lesbians is arguably not just another human rights violation, lamentable as it may be, but a calculated way of portraying Russia as the spearhead against western decadence, evident especially in the West's tolerant embrace of homosexuality. According to Robert Cottrell, stigmatizing homosexuality is a way for Putin's stagnating regime to mobilize popular support against the permissive West.[13] And Brian Taylor notes that Putin's homophobia, putatively a reflection of his macho toughness, resonates well with ordinary Russians.[14]

Cottrell makes his point in a review essay taking off from Masha Gessens's *The Future is History: How Totalitarianism Reclaimed Russia* (2017), which we considered briefly in chapter 1 as an example of promiscuous usage. Cottrell agrees that Gessen uses the term too loosely, but his own characterizations, in citing Dugin, raise other questions.[15] As Cottrell sees it,

> Dugin wants his Russian world to be totalitarian, which is to say, a world in which the state polices everybody's thoughts as well as everybody's actions. He opposes universal human

rights and the rule of law as alien ideas from the hostile West. Gessen claims in her title that Russia is already totalitarian. I imagine that Dugin would disagree. And from a different perspective, so would I.[16]

Even the Russian police, Cottrell insists, do not operate in a totalitarian way. And in arguing that Putin's Russia is authoritarian as opposed to totalitarian, Cottrell brings in North Korea and its dictatorial leader Kim Jong-un for comparison: "Putin wants all Russians to think like him, whereas Kim Jong-un would rather his subjects not think at all."[17]

This is surely an arresting way of making a key distinction, but we need not choose between Gessen and Cottrell because each is thinking in terms of an unnecessarily delimited notion of totalitarianism. Before considering the alternative, however, we must further consider the place of ideology. Whereas some see Putin as subject to ideologues, others portray him as an improviser, moving somewhere between opportunism and pragmatism. According to Mikhail Zygar, "It is logic that Putin-era Russia lacks. The chain of events ... reveals the absence of a clear plan or strategy on the part of Putin himself or his courtiers. Everything that happens is a tactical step, a real-time response to external stimuli devoid of an ultimate objective."[18]

Brian Taylor's dissection of the "code of Putinism" offers a nuanced alternative to both coherent ideology and self-serving pragmatism. Putin, Taylor argues, operates in terms of a code that is at once more and less than an ideology, that includes emotions and habits as well as ideas. The three intersect in ways that give the code coherence beyond any one element. Indeed, it is the overlap and blurring of elements that makes it a coherent code or mentality.[19] And the litany of slights in international affairs has been experienced as it has – as disrespect, humiliation – partly because of the code, which is deeper and has other sources than those slights themselves.

Taylor concedes that many of Putin's criticisms of US foreign policy have been warranted and widely shared, yet the code led Putin and the Russians to magnify US mistakes. A bit later Taylor lays out the implications even more pointedly: "What the United States calls democracy promotion, Russia regards as externally sponsored attempts at regime change. The interaction of the code of Putinism with American tendencies toward sanctimoniousness about the universality of its liberal and democratic values and its perceived benign role in the world produces a particularly combustible mix."[20]

In any case, as Taylor sees it, Putin did not set out to create an authoritarian dictatorship, but concern for the strength of the state and for maintaining control led in that direction.[21] Taylor does not use the totalitarianism category but refers instead to electoral authoritarianism or authoritarian dictatorship. Nevertheless, his analysis can significantly illuminate the applicability of totalitarianism to Putin's Russia.

The Russian economy under Putin recalls those of the two fascist regimes up to a point. We have seen that some find the continuance of private ownership of the means of production under the fascist regimes a warrant for distinguishing them from the Soviet Union, whatever the overlap in methods of governance. But there are many modes of relationship between the political and economic spheres even in capitalist systems, and Putin's Russia, like Mussolini's Italy and Hitler's Germany, has departed significantly from the free market in statist, interventionist directions.

Though Russia remains nominally a capitalist system, Taylor features the state's control over "the commanding heights of the economy." For Putin, the economy was too important to be left alone, so he entrusted key parts to trusted members of his circle.

It was a totalitarian statist move when from the outset Putin set out to subordinate big business, which thought it had taken over the state under Boris Yeltsin, his predecessor as president. The weakness of formal capitalist institutions, especially the rule of law and protections for private property, then enabled state officials to determine winners and losers, outside the parameters of market competition. Moreover, property rights in the most important sectors remain merely provisional. The economic oligarchs recognize that they are subject to the will of the state, that they must do whatever Putin says, even give up their property if necessary for political reasons.[22] That, especially, recalls the fascist relationship between the state and big business and, if anything, constitutes a further statist step. Private property is not an absolute right but must serve the national interest.

Yet Taylor also features the weakness and ineffectiveness of the Russian state under Putin. The neutering of the formal checks and balances leaves the informal clans the only counterweights. And the combination of hyper-presidentialism and informal clan competition is inevitably an ineffective form of governance: "Putinism, with its reliance on informal networks over formal institutions, and with the preference for loyalty over competence, means that the Russian state remains highly ineffective, in spite of Putin's pretensions to be the great state-builder."[23]

Weakness and ineffectiveness might seem to suggest anything but totalitarianism. Yet it is by now well established that the earlier totalitarian regimes, and especially the two fascist powers, were never the strong, monolithic, unified states they appeared to some at the time. They too had their fiefdoms. But the element of "feudalism," the hollowing out of the state, seems considerably greater in Putin's Russia.

The key difference, however, is not this weakness of the state but the greater degree of fear and mistrust in Putin's Russia. As Taylor sees it, the dominant belief is the need for a strong state to protect Russia against internal and external enemies. This reflects a deep distrust of spontaneity and uncontrolled behavior. Control is essential given the weakness of others – including weaker states. If we do not control them, someone else will.[24]

Putin's Russia has seen a modicum of mobilization around patriotic themes, especially the image of Russia spearheading a civilizational alternative to the West, but there has been greater concern with control than mobilization. For all their insistence on a leadership stratum, the three earlier totalitarian regimes, like China and even Iran, engaged in such mobilization based on greater confidence in the potential of ordinary people. According to the code of Putinism, ordinary Russians would always need to be controlled; the aim was not to raise them to a new level.

On the matter of defensiveness, we note a symptomatic difference between Taylor and Gerard Toal. To be sure, their accounts run parallel up to a point because each features the place of emotion against conventional western emphases on ideology, pragmatic power politics, or some abiding Russian imperialism. But Toal has more room for positive aims and relies less on mere defensiveness in explaining Russia's interventions in Georgia and Ukraine. Rather than fear and state security concerns, he features pride, glory, righteous indignation, the protection of ethnic kinship, and the power of emotional ties to particular places.[25]

In that light, Toal disputes the widespread view that a neo-imperial insistence on a sphere of influence on Russia's borders is the key to Putin's behavior.[26] For Taylor, in contrast, it is almost self-evident that Putin wants above all to upend western claims about the rights of Russia's near neighbors to choose their own foreign policy, independent of Russian tutelage. Conversely, he wants the West to recognize a Russian sphere of influence in the former Soviet space.[27] Insofar as Toal is featuring *common* emotional ties among Russians, his reading, more than Taylor's, suggests mobilizing and thus totalitarian potential.

In any case, Putin's Russia is by no means merely an old-fashioned authoritarian regime or personal dictatorship. Nor is it merely capitalism plus authoritarianism but rather transcends the combination in a way that points toward totalitarianism in some respects. But the degree of fear and defensiveness severely limits the totalitarian potential. Though we found a shadow of shrillness, vulnerability, and self-doubt in the earlier totalitarian regimes, they evidenced greater confidence, buoyancy, and hubris than we find in Putin's Russia.

China under Xi Jinping

In the last chapter, I noted that some see a return to totalitarianism in China with the recent rise of Xi Jinping, who was already general secretary of the Chinese Communist Party and president of the People's Republic of China before being designated "core leader" in 2016. In an editorial of February 2018, the *Washington Post* warned that "forgetting the lessons of Mao's often disastrous reign, Xi is attempting to construct a 21st-century model of totalitarianism and offer it as an example to the rest of the world."[28] This warning was triggered by the recent announcement that presidential term limits would be removed from the constitution, so that Xi could conceivably remain president for life. As the *Post* saw it, this ended the collective leadership that Deng had fostered and that had made for an orderly transition in the top leadership every ten years, thus avoiding any cult of personality.

Whereas that in itself would not have constituted totalitarianism, the *Post* mentioned several other significant steps that, especially taken together, might indeed suggest a return to totalitarianism. Xi clamped down on the internet and on criticism overall; he arrested human rights lawyers; he pushed a social credit system for rewarding or punishing all Chinese citizens; and he fostered the so-called Belt and Road Initiative to extend Chinese influence, first across Asia but then on to Africa and Europe. By 2019, anyone would add the renewed reliance on "re-education centers," targeting especially ethnic separatists and minority religious groups.

Although she features many of the same steps, Elizabeth Economy does not push the notion of a return to totalitarianism. But she emphasizes the sense of crisis and contradiction in the Chinese communist regime by the time Xi rose to power.[29] There had been a loss of ideological coherence. Party membership had become merely a means to personal advancement. Despite its economic successes, the regime was not keeping up in providing public goods like health care and a clean environment.

Xi was determined to change course and rejuvenate China. In light of the perceived challenge, three prongs were fundamental: first, to revivify the party and the ideology and give the state a more active role; second, to minimize access to competing ideas; and third, to galvanize popular enthusiasm for large-scale enterprises suggesting national greatness.

Corruption, undermining the people's confidence in the party, seemed the greatest immediate threat so Xi launched a concerted anti-corruption campaign in 2012. It remained ongoing as of 2019. Entailing the sort of reciprocity that we found earlier, the campaign relies on mobilizing the public to report abuses by government officials. It has been serious, extensive, and seemingly effective up to a point. Still, it has also involved arbitrariness, including favoritism to loyalists and a lack of due process. With so many being targeted, economic efficiency has suffered, partly because officials become cautious, unsure about changing rules.[30]

In light of concern about diminishing ideological belief, the leadership has played up Marxism and the socialist nature of the Chinese system, despite the continuing importance of market mechanisms. Conversely, fear of liberal ideas has increased, as has pressure on the universities to inculcate socialist values. Ideological education quickly became a hallmark of Xi's leadership. At the same time, the government imposed new limits on the Chinese media and even on international non-governmental organizations.[31]

Central to the overall effort has been increased exploitation of social media – for surveillance and control, on the one hand, and for indoctrination, on the other. China first acquired a public internet service in 1995, and immediately the government understood the unique combination of advantages and dangers it presented. It might serve as a governmental tool, most obviously for surveillance and for keeping informed of public opinion, but also for mobilization. However, such new technologies seemed inherently to diffuse power so they might prove destabilizing, eroding the regime's authority. From the start, the government sought both to reach citizens through the internet as well as to control the speech that occurred there.[32]

Ostensibly to protect Chinese users from harmful content, especially originating from abroad, the government soon developed its "great firewall," blocking not only criticism of leaders but for the most part Google, Facebook, YouTube, and Twitter altogether. As the government came to recognize how it could exploit the internet, it softened its stance somewhat. But Xi's revitalization effort has resulted in a further crackdown, with deeper restrictions and what some call an internet army to monitor content.[33]

The stepped-up surveillance has seemed especially significant because of a new social credit scoring system for companies and individuals, entailing both punishment and reward and intended to be fully implemented by 2020. Its backbone is the National Credit Information Sharing Platform established in 2015, soon supported by an integrated human-monitoring system involving public surveillance cameras. By 2018, China had nearly two hundred million of them, far more than any other country, and it announced the goal of making them omnipresent by 2020. The system gives users a score based on surveillance of their activities, on and off line. They might lose points for traffic violations, for example, or for spreading rumors online, or for buying the wrong things, or for wasting their free time. People with high scores are given special opportunities, including access to jobs, loans, and travel.[34]

Many Chinese find the system appropriate but to critics this innovation, especially, has seemed totalitarian. As Economy puts it, in her only use of the totalitarianism category, "Some Chinese express concerns about the totalitarian nature of the social-credit program."[35] Alexander Klimburg characterizes the social credit plan as Orwellian, noting that combined with social media it portends a nightmarishly effective mode of social control.[36] However, the social credit system has so far proven relatively gentle and less intrusive than the virtuocracy that Susan Shirk attributed to Mao's effort, as we saw in the preceding chapter. It is not as if everybody is expected to exceed production targets to get a good score. The imperative is simply to do what is expected, in a relatively low-level sense, and not to make trouble. And the punishments envisioned to this point do not remotely approximate the Gulag or concentration camp.

In light of the renewed emphasis on Marxism and socialism, Xi has been especially concerned with the state sector of the economy. But though he has made a passing effort to improve the efficiency of state-owned enterprises (SOEs), more striking has been the increasing pressure from the government to make them serve the regime's wider political aims, such as lifetime employment, and its strategic objectives abroad where, as "national champions," they are to carry China's name in international competition. Despite advantages from the government, however, the SOEs notoriously underperform private firms.[37] Such economic efficiency, however, is not remotely a criterion of totalitarianism.

Though the results have been mixed, the Xi government's war on pollution, declared in 2014 and intended to address not only China's notorious air pollution but environmental degradation more generally, has been more serious than the effort to reform the SOEs. In a sense, in fact, this environmental effort can be considered as itself a totalitarian great task, mobilizing the population. Ordinary citizens might report on a polluting factory, so that government regulators could then crack down. Or citizens might even take a polluter to court. Such responses, however, were to support, not question, official policy.[38]

Whereas the anti-pollution effort has been widely welcomed, a feature of Xi's China that has received a good deal of unfavorable attention in the West is the renewed reliance, noted above, on mind control through re-education centers. This has primarily targeted ethnic separatists and minority religious groups, especially the Muslim Uighurs in Xinjiang, a large but relatively isolated province in the northwest part of the country. The program came to light outside the region only in 2017, after Elizabeth Economy had finished her book. There were thought to be 1,200 such camps confining as many as a million people as of early 2019.[39]

In terms of ethnic policy, the communist regime was reasonably pluralistic at first, largely following the Soviet example in a comparably multi-ethnic empire. But the collapse of the Soviet Union led to reassessment. The degree of pluralism in Soviet nationality policy seemed a significant source of the collapse. From there, the Chinese communists increasingly emphasized Han assimilationism and demonized religion as itself contrary to unitary pan-Chinese identity.[40]

But even during the earlier period of relative pluralism, the communist regime had been particularly intolerant of distinctive Uighur religious practices, which included a measure of Sufi mysticism. However, the new "re-education" effort went considerably further, insisting that the Uighurs disavow Islam and their "backward" culture.[41] This campaign provoked a backlash among the Uighurs, leading some to embrace radical Islamic Salafist ideas from outside. One result has been periodic terrorism, and thus James Millward concedes that the Chinese government has legitimate concerns about Uighur unrest. But he concludes that China has exaggerated the threat and responded excessively, with a heavy police presence and a vast surveillance apparatus, in addition to the re-education program.[42]

This effort to re-educate the Uighurs is surely a quintessentially totalitarian practice, reflecting an absolute intolerance of pluralism and separate identity. Still, the relatively restricted range of the suppression is significant. To be sure, anyone challenging the regime, and not only religious minorities, may be subject to re-education, but the vast majority of Chinese citizens can simply go about their business if they choose. And for targeted groups the aim is full assimilation, not elimination by whatever form of ethnic cleansing. But though the re-education program does not itself make the regime totalitarian overall, it does indicate an ongoing potential.

In the preceding chapter, we noted that Timothy Cheek, writing in 2010, found a retreat from totalitarianism in contrast to the ideological fervor that Mao had demanded. Just a few years later, however, Wenfang Tang played up the expectation of almost constant involvement in local and national politics. Ordinary people were to review, comment on, and possibly reject what the party put forward. Tang noted that a good deal of interpersonal trust was necessary to underpin this political activism and high-risk collective action.[43]

Although ordinary people successfully denounced local abuses and corruption, perhaps their most surprising influence has been on foreign policy, usually in pushing perceived Chinese national interests. On occasion, the government has adopted a proactive approach to encourage popular protest in light of perceived slights from abroad. But sometimes, manifesting popular nationalism, the people press for a harder line than the regime would like, especially in dealing with Japan, Taiwan, North Korea, and the United States. A key example is the ongoing dispute with Japan over islands in the East China Sea. The regime relies partly on its nationalist credentials for legitimacy so it is especially reluctant to repress foreign policy discontents.[44]

And indeed the great task under Xi is the drive for Chinese preeminence in the world, no longer simply to be competitive and accepted as a major player, as under Deng and his successors. China seeks the higher profile that it believes its economic success warrants, and China's accelerated pace has had particular resonance as the country asserts itself after an earlier century of humiliation.

On the domestic level, Xi and the leadership recognize that though China's workforce has become globally competitive on the basis of skills, no longer primarily low wages, China has continued to lag in technological innovation. In an effort to propel the country to the forefront, Xi launched an ambitious "Made in China 2025" program targeting ten high technology sectors for rapid development, ideally to lead to Chinese preeminence. But the limited success of the effort to move to the forefront in developing electric cars did not bode well.[45]

On the international level, China has sought to expand its reach across Asia and the Middle East into Africa and Europe. Through such institutions as the Asian Infrastructure Investment Bank, it invests in infrastructure and seeks to promote economic integration. The overall thrust is summed up as the Belt and Road Initiative, first unveiled in 2013, intended to become a network of highways, railways, and ports. Deliberately recalling the old Silk Road, which made China central to a vast international trade network, the historical resonances of the Belt and Road Initiative give it an almost mythical status among many Chinese scholars and officials.[46] However, other Chinese remain unconvinced, and by 2018 some of the foreign leaders initially eager to partner with China were becoming restive with Chinese leadership, which had come to appear too obviously self-serving.

Though the results remain mixed, China under Xi has taken steps usefully considered totalitarian. And it is surely closer than contemporary Russia or Iran to totalitarianism. More assertive and less merely defensive, China is making a more concerted, coherent effort at grandiose, mobilizing initiatives.

Western observers like Economy typically remain skeptical about the viability of Chinese ventures, citing especially political limitations, with western liberal democracy taken to be the standard. They stress that even as the Chinese seek to innovate and aspire to global leadership, they cling to political objectives that compromise efficiency. Above all, the Chinese are caught up in a tension between their insistence on control of information and the need for a free flow of information for economic innovation.[47]

This line of argument is convincing up to a point. But the same sort of argument has been applied to China for decades, and the Chinese economy has undeniably accomplished a great deal under China's unforeseen, still nominally communist, political system. In the same vein, western observers are quick to see unrest or protest as evidence that the communist regime is in crisis. But Wenfang Tang argues convincingly that even widespread protest does not indicate declining support and the coming of democracy; in fact, the Communist Party has strong support in all reaches of society.[48] Continued liberal triumphalism may compromise our capacity to assess China's prospects, even its renewed totalitarian directions.

The editors of an important recent book on China's internet policy observe astutely that what we find in China is not merely oscillation between relaxation and control because the dynamism of technology yields a more complex, constantly changing picture.[49] More generally, they note that "simple dichotomies of 'freedom versus control' or 'promoting democracy versus strengthening authoritarianism' do not suffice as frameworks for understanding the role and impact of new media in today's China."[50]

Quite apart from the media, we clearly must transcend the conventional dichotomies in considering contemporary China. Teresa Wright provocatively suggests that the system the Chinese have developed is in some ways more "democratic" than the conventional democracies of the West. The key, she contends, is not the system itself but the attitude and ability of the leaders. If they are pragmatic, competent, and reasonably responsive, freedom from election can actually make them more effective. And if they need not worry about attracting donors and getting re-elected, they can seek what is best in the longer term. Although corruption remains a problem, for the most part post-Mao leaders have been pragmatic and competent.[51]

In a similar vein, Tang notes that the mass line entails a kind of direct democracy, connecting the state with the people, often bypassing administrative regulations and legal procedures. And in pursuing the policy, the regime responds to public demands more quickly than democracies typically do, and the Chinese are more likely than those in democratic societies to find government responsive. This explains the strong support the regime has continued to enjoy. But Tang also points out, as the other side of the coin, that this direct link has deleterious implication for intermediary civic organizations and the rule of law.[52]

In making such arguments, neither Wright nor Tang is remotely recommending the Chinese system over western-style democracy but simply suggesting that in approaching China we must get beyond either/or, with stereotypical notions of democracy and authoritarianism (or totalitarianism) as the alternatives. Most basically, it is necessary to consider the Chinese case from an alternative point of view to see why western observers have found it so hard to understand the surprising degree of consensus that attaches to the undemocratic Chinese regime, even as it becomes more totalitarian.

The Islamic world

Although the earlier totalitarian potential in Iran seems to have dissipated, despite periodic waves of repression, radical Islamism with totalitarian potential has remained important in other parts of the Islamic world. More than anything done by the Islamic Republic of Iran, the brief reign of the Taliban in Afghanistan, from 1996–2001, when it controlled more than 75 percent of the country, brought home to the world the potential of Islamic extremism on the domestic level. This was especially through the regime's harsh interpretation and strict enforcement of sharia law, which particularly restricted women. The regime was also widely condemned, in the Muslim world as elsewhere, for its destruction of monuments deemed idolatrous, including a pair of massive Buddha statues that had stood, carved into a mountainside, for 1,500 years.

The Taliban regime was routed by a US-led NATO coalition in the wake of the 2001 terrorist attacks on the United States. But the Taliban regrouped thereafter and, as of 2019, remained a major force contending for power in war-torn Afghanistan. But most troubling in terms of the totalitarianism question has been the Islamic State (IS), which grew from the ISIS with the proclamation of a new caliphate under Abu Bakr al-Baghdadi in 2014.

The movement had emerged from within a radical Islamist network that was international virtually from its origins. It arose to resist the attempted Soviet takeover of Afghanistan in the 1980s. The struggle attracted many young Muslims, especially from the Arab world. Among them was the Jordanian Abu Musab al-Zarqawi, who by the late 1990s had become the leading figure in a shadowy terrorist network. The US invasion of Iraq, beginning in March 2003, and the subsequent US victory and occupation especially facilitated the development of his movement.

The Sunni clerical establishment in Iraq was almost uniformly hostile to the American occupation, though welcomed its impact in fostering Islamization, a sense that radical change in an Islamist direction was imperative.[53] By 2004, Zarqawi was gaining renown among Iraqi Sunnis as the fiercest foe of the American occupation.[54] His recruiting videos promised not only the liberation of Islamic lands but also a new world order, the ultimate triumph of Islam in a new caliphate. The Zarqawi network was in and out of favor with al-Qaeda and thus went by varying names, but the two groups ultimately diverged acrimoniously in 2013, largely over tactical matters.

In 2006, Zarqawi was himself killed in a targeted American airstrike, but his disciples, now calling themselves the Islamic State in Iraq, carried on. However, with the situation in Iraq stabilizing somewhat after the American troop surge of 2007, the Islamic State in Iraq barely managed to survive. Though engaging in occasional terror, it was seemingly becoming an irrelevant sideshow. In 2010, Abu Bakr al-Baghdadi, a scholar with a doctoral degree and a professor of Islamic law, emerged as leader.

Then in 2011 dramatic turns in both Iraq and Syria enhanced the possibilities. In Iraq, the American occupation ended with the withdrawal of American troops, but sectarian divisions bedeviled the new Iraqi order. The Shia-led government's policies provoked Sunni resentment, and many Sunnis were prepared to support an Islamist anti-government alternative. Meanwhile, in Syria "Arab Spring" protests against the regime of Bashar al-Assad soon led to civil war.

The Baghdadi group abolished a rival organization in 2013 and proclaimed themselves the Islamic State in Iraq and Syria (ISIS), also known as the Islamic State in Iraq and the Levant (ISIL) and in Arabic as *Daesh*. Zarqawi was credited as the key forerunner and, despite the confusing name changes, he is widely seen as the founder of ISIS and its successor, IS.

By 2013, ISIS was very much on the offensive. It became an actual state as it took over the Syrian city of Raqqa from Syrian insurgents later that year. Proclaimed the capital of the new state, Raqqa was the first city to undergo ISIS rule. In characterizing both the ideology and functioning of the Islamic State, Ahmed Hashim was more willing than most to use the language of totalitarianism: "The Islamic State's ideology is totalistic and uncompromising and sees the world in black and white; it is dangerous and revolutionary."[55] And he goes on:

> A particularly insidious aspect of the strategies of state-formation and nation-building is a process that can be referred to as cultural or "pathological" "homogenization," defined as a sustained effort to wipe out all vestiges of the historical past that are in conflict with the building party's ideological views, to eradicate or expel groups of people or individuals who are portrayed as the enemy, and to instill a system of total control over the people... .[56]

And certainly the ISIS program in Raqqa must be considered one archetypal form of totalitarianism. The new regime carried out grisly executions, closed Christian churches, and blew up the local Shiite mosque in its campaign to terrorize, kill, or expel minority groups. But by establishing Islamic schools and imposing mandatory religious observances and sharia law, it also enforced ideological homogenization on those deemed to belong. There were bans on smoking and drinking, western music, and displays of western clothing in shop windows. Women could leave home only if fully covered. In schools, western notions like nation-state, democracy, and rationalism could not even be discussed. Policing was intense as the new state entrenched itself in the daily lives of the residents. Transgressions were dealt with swiftly, often on the spot.

According to Hashim, the regime had "established a totalitarian system of 'busybodies' with a network of informants and agent provocateurs. This totalitarian police force scared most inhabitants into resigned acceptance of IS's control in the urban areas." Yet, especially in the beginning, when the regime had plenty of money and faced no external military pressure, it devoted considerable effort to maintaining essential services.[57]

During 2014, IS seized control of a third of Iraqi territory. Early that year, ISIS captured its first Iraq town, Falujah, with the support of disaffected Sunnis. Then in June 2014 it stunned the world by taking Mosul, Iraq's second-largest city. The conquests included banks, oil wells, and seemingly all that the new state would need to remain an ongoing concern. In Falujah and Mosel, as in Raqqa, the regime implemented extreme Islamist measures, including sharia law.

In June 2014, from a noted mosque in Mosul, Baghdadi proclaimed the new state a caliphate, after the ruling council had elected Baghdadi himself as caliph. This was putatively a worldwide caliphate to which all Muslims owed allegiance, and as such it would be called simply the Islamic State (IS), no longer limited to Iraq and Syria. This was a bold move, offering a promise of religious unity that many Muslims welcomed. But other Muslims objected. Al-Qaeda, for example, had believed that such a caliphate could be created only after the secular rulers in the Islamic world had been toppled. Baghdadi, in contrast, held that once the caliphate had been established, Muslims would fall in line and overcome the apostate secular regimes.[58] Certainly, the new state's message of fighting for something bigger than Iraq and Syria proved effective. Over the next couple of years, it attracted volunteers from 50 countries.

But the radical lineage from Zarqawi to Baghdadi had provoked significant opposition from within the Islamic world all along. During 2004–5, Jordan's King Abdullah sponsored what came to be called the Amman Message, which rejected religiously inspired violence and denounced tactics like Zarqawi's. King Abdullah then got the message widely endorsed by Muslim scholars.[59] When IS proclaimed a worldwide caliphate, many, including leading Sunni theologians, objected vociferously, disputing the very legitimacy of IS. Among them was Qatar-based Yusuf al-Qaradawi, whom we encountered in chapter 4 as the heir to Sayyid Qtub and perhaps the most influential spokesman for radical Islam. He insisted that the title of caliph could be bestowed only by the entire Muslim community, not by a single group, so the IS caliphate was void under sharia – and dangerous.

Still, IS continued to expand militarily, taking control of a large area in western Iraq and eastern Syria by December 2015. At that point, it controlled an area the size of Britain and seemed poised even to capture Baghdad, leading to the collapse of the Iraqi state. IS had become notorious for releasing videos of beheadings and other executions, even of journalists and aid workers. And, like the Taliban, it destroyed cultural heritage sites it considered offensive to Islam.

But IS arguably fell into typically totalitarian overreach, which produced serious problems even before a coalition of forces began coming together in 2016, seeking to oust it militarily. The extreme measures in Falujah and Mosel came to alienate many local Sunnis who had initially supported the regime against the Shiite-dominated Iraqi government.[60] By the end of 2016, IS was also losing support because it was no longer providing services effectively. Even in 2015 it was beginning to face recruitment problems. Hashim concludes that in light of the pressures on resources, consolidation of the territory won would likely have worked better than the ideologically fueled drive for expansion. In short, IS bit off more than it could chew. It lacked the resources to build a state and fight at the same time, and its ideological rigidities alienated those it ruled.[61]

IS progressively forfeited territory during 2016–17 and was left without a territorial base early in 2019. But with its totalitarian aspiration and potential, it arguably remained the spearhead of radical Islam. Partly in compensation for its setbacks, IS stepped up its global terrorism effort, engineering a major attack on Paris, its first on a western capital, in November 2015. Through such terrorism, the militants sought to foment a backlash against Muslims in the West, forcing them to choose.[62]

At the same time, most observers agree that as long as the

situation is unsettled in Iraq and Syria, IS will remain poised for a comeback. In a recent assessment of Iraqi policy in the aftermath of the IS defeat, the *New Yorker* writer Ben Taub concluded that the draconian official revenge, targeting, without due process, anyone who even knew the families of ISIS or IS members, almost guarantees such a comeback: "Hundreds of thousands of civilians are suffering at the hands of their liberators. Anyone with a perceived connection to isis [sic], however tenuous or unclear, is being killed or cast out of society." This has not been merely an assault on ISIS but a Shiite assault on Sunnis. So the caliphate lives on as a fantasy of Islamic justice and governance measured against the corrupt reality of the Iraqi state.[63]

The scope for further totalitarian departures

In pondering the scope for totalitarianism in the future, we must also consider whether some still newer form might emerge, whether in the western mainstream or outside it, in response to sociopolitical challenges already evident. Writing in the early 1990s, concluding a notable analysis of the overall Soviet experiment, Martin Malia found it unlikely that the failure of that experiment would end the totalitarian impulse. As for what might feed a new totalitarian politics, Malia pointed to the "South–North" conflict, to ecological concerns, and to the aspirations fueling contemporary liberation movements. Genuine problems were at issue in each case. Perhaps, Malia concluded, the Soviet outcome would inoculate us against extreme responses, but should a contingent, unforeseen crisis comparable to World War I befall us, there was no telling what might happen.[64]

The rise of Islamic extremism surely counts as an instance of "South–North" conflict. With the concern over global warming, it is now even easier to envision environmental problems generating a totalitarian response. Or such a departure might be triggered by a concern for security in light of terrorist threats or even by some extraterrestrial menace. Such nightmare scenarios would enhance the likelihood that new modes of societal mobilization, manipulation, and surveillance would seem necessary – and would even be welcomed by most. But even if welcomed initially, those modes might invite systematic abuse.

The totalitarian potential of new technologies

By now, images of a renewed totalitarianism seem bound to encompass new technologies. Such innovations as facial recognition software, genetic profiling, and genetic engineering raise alarms, but concerns have surfaced especially over the cyber revolution that has brought us computers and the interconnectivity of computers through the internet. From there, we have seen the advent of social media such as Facebook, Twitter, and YouTube. The possibility that any message will "go viral" indicates the scope for reaching very large numbers of people virtually instantaneously. At the same time, our smartphones track our locations through global positioning satellites.

For the most part, however, the internet and social media have seemed notably positive innovations, their advantages self-evident. They serve freedom, pluralism, individual autonomy; they facilitate free inquiry; and they foster communication, possibly even enhancing the scope for democratic change. One Facebook executive famously boasted that Facebook connects people which, he insisted, is desirable in itself. Yet it has seemed that the panoply of new technologies might prove readily subverted by governments, corporations, just plain "bad actors," or some combination, thereby making possible more comprehensive modes of surveillance and control, on the one hand, and of mobilization, manipulation, and disinformation, on the other.

We have seen that both Russia and China have harnessed the internet and social media for purposes that suggest such wider totalitarian potential. Slavoj Žižek included "digitalization" and concerns about privacy among the reasons for current worries about a return to totalitarianism.[65] In the same vein, Tzetvan Todorov noted that even modern democracies have scientific tools, like surveillance and the genetic code, that make the means available to earlier totalitarians seem prehistoric.[66]

It is certainly true that these technologies seem to erode the public–private distinction, which might seem worrisome on the face of it. As we discussed in chapter 3, challenging that distinction was one key to the earlier totalitarian direction. But even insofar as the internet and social media also point in that direction, for the most part their advantages have seemed to outweigh any disadvantages. The loss of privacy is simply the other side of the connectivity that we value. A good example of the trade-off is the so-called Internet of Things (IoT), which enhances convenience and efficiency by connecting everyday objects such as microchipped clothing and smart appliances. But it also generates information about what had formerly been utterly private activities, so it has the potential for abuse, depending how the user's identity, location, and activities are treated.

The internet has seemed to promote freedom and pluralism partly because it evolved in a dispersed, even chaotic, fashion, and many seek to keep it from centralized control by anyone, especially governments. This contrasts with the "internet sovereignty" that both Russia and China advocate, as we have seen. As to which of the two models is more likely to head off abuse, there is disagreement partly, but only partly, because of disagreement over what constitutes abuse. But even insofar as we find the potential for abuse, we must ask what it has to do with totalitarianism. When systematically misused, social media have often sown confusion and chaos, which is anything but totalitarian in itself, even if perpetrated by the Russians or the Chinese.

Complicating assessment is the fact that terms like "Orwellian" and "surveillance state" are often used to indicate the dangers. To some extent, these serve as stand-ins for totalitarianism, but the relationships are ambiguous or uncertain. Some emphasize that Orwell's dystopia in *Nineteen Eighty-Four* has come to seem quaintly old-fashioned in light of the possibilities for surveillance and manipulation now available. At the same time, we have noted that what Orwell offered was to some extent a caricature of totalitarianism. So whether "Orwellian" is more, or less, appropriate than "totalitarian" to characterize abuses and dangers is not obvious.

Although discussion has focused almost exclusively on the potential for abuse, in principle the new technology could serve what some, at least, might take as the positive side of a totalitarian venture. And indeed Alexander Klimburg notes the striking Soviet interest, by the later 1940s, in the ideas of Norbert Wiener, the father of cybernetics, which the Soviets viewed as an inherently communist tool for total planning and resource allocation. Even the computer itself they found quintessentially communist.[67] Whatever we think of the possibilities for economic planning, the Soviet communists were not envisioning simply an enhanced instrument for surveillance and control.

The most obvious targets of concern today are governments – not only those like China and Russia outside the western mainstream but also democratic governments with the potential for abuse that might place democracy itself at risk. As for what might prompt such misuses of the new technologies, we need not look very far. It is not surprising that response to the ongoing threat of terrorism after the September 2001 attack on the United States fueled a major enhancement in governmental cyber capabilities. And the potential for misuse seems to remain, whether within the ongoing "war on terror" or outside it. Such misuse would not necessarily be by government in general; it could be by those specialized governmental entities with greatest access to the information. The fear is, first, that surveillance itself can have a chilling effect and then, above all, that the information gathered could be weaponized against the country's own citizens to serve some particular agenda.

Even as he criticizes internet policy in Russia and China, Klimburg discerns a more general danger as he considers how government entities have come to use cyber in the United States. At issue is especially "strategic communication," which concerns government uses of cyber for intelligence gathering. Klimburg indicates several instances of US government agencies issuing half-truths and innuendo on the internet in an effort to obfuscate, to hide what they were doing from the public.[68] The temptation for governments to use on their own citizens the technological means that were developed for use against foreign entities is perhaps irresistible. Klimburg draws a sobering conclusion: "The danger is that left on its own, strategic communication will mutate into full-blown Russian- and Chinese-style information warfare: a consistent and willful distortion of narrative aimed at influencing the adversary's decision making, where the adversary includes one's own citizens and the conflict is permanent."[69] We might add that if the conflict is permanent, any of the contending parties would be tempted to cement permanent partisan advantage through totalitarian methods enabled by the internet.

Tamsin Shaw feels that Klimburg is so hung up on the potential for governmental abuse that he plays down the scope for malfeasance by private high-tech companies, especially "the big five": Microsoft, Apple, Facebook, Amazon, and Google.[70] For Shaw, it is worrisome when such companies, individually or in combination, work with the US government on national security matters, as the quest for security seems liable to compromise privacy. But Shaw's deepest concern is not the collusion itself but the willingness of the government to surrender unprecedented power to such private, profit-making companies: "Extensive control of information has been handed over to unaccountable global corporations that don't profit from the truth." As a result, Shaw goes on, we find ourselves "heavily reliant on the goodwill of a handful of billionaires. They are, and will continue to be, responsible for maintaining the public's confidence in information, preserving forms of credibility that are necessary for the health and success of our liberal democratic institutions."[71]

The concern is not necessarily with government, on the one hand, and tech companies on the other, as if they should be clearly distinguished. They may intertwine, and insofar as they do, they arguably create still greater potential for abuse. Shaw is concerned about something like a new iteration of "the military–industrial complex," though this new technology complex is more dangerous because it can collect and analyze massive amounts of data. Thus the scope not only for keeping tabs on individuals but for manipulating and mobilizing whole populations. These companies have at their disposal, in Shaw's words, "the most sophisticated tools of persuasion humans have ever devised."[72] This surely implies the potential for something like totalitarianism.

Up to a point, the danger is less that firms like Facebook and Twitter themselves become perpetrators than that they become vehicles for the malfeasance of others. Even that is a fuzzy line, however, for the firms are sometimes at least semi-complicit, as when Cambridge Analytica, a UK-based political consultancy that worked on Donald Trump's 2016 US presidential campaign, obtained from Facebook information on millions of users, without their consent, to enable the consultancy to micro-target messages to voters. Facebook was not taking a political stand but was seemingly willing to the sell the data it had "harvested" to anyone for whatever purpose.

On other occasions, these firms were more obviously unknowing vehicles, as when, also during the 2016 US presidential campaign, Russian trolls and bots – fake accounts disguised as legitimate clients – used Google, Facebook, and Twitter to spread disinformation. At that point, these companies had few mechanisms for determining the reliability of the information they made available. And they have generally resisted efforts to make them accountable for the content disseminated through their platforms, on the plausible grounds that they are not censors.

Siva Vaidhyanathan has recently offered a sustained attack on Facebook in particular, though he finds some of the same problems with Google. The problem is not only that Facebook gathers personal information used for selling ads, information that has also been used for government surveillance. Nor is it that Facebook lets in Russian bots that spread disinformation. The more basic worry, as he sees it, is that Facebook fosters habits of mind among its users that are inimical to democracy. What we post is more about identity and social bonding than truth. So we favor highly charged content that tends to promote polarization and tribal divisions. Facebook use undermines not only rational deliberation but confidence in the very possibility of rational deliberation and debate. At the same time, Facebook offers a means of intimidating harassment, which may lead us to back off from sharing our views at all.[73]

Undermining democracy is bad enough, but Vaidhyanathan

worries explicitly that doing so may open the way to authoritarianism.[74] Although his baseline notion of how democracy has worked, based on rational deliberation and the like, seems a bit idealized, Vaidhyanathan has pinpointed a genuine danger. Nonetheless, drawing out the implications of his account makes it clear that such an erosion of democracy would not itself portend totalitarianism but, at least at first, something closer to its opposite – division, fragmentation, polarization, the erosion of common standards and of our trust in institutions, expertise, and each other. The antithesis of totalitarianism is something like anarchy or libertarian individualism; it is certainly not democracy, which requires a measure of coherence and commonality – just not the extreme degree sought by totalitarians. In principle, of course, the ungovernability that could result from the erosion of democracy might provoke a turn toward totalitarianism as an antidote.

The cyber world presents the potential for abuse partly because of vulnerability to hacking – breaking into the computers of others by governments, private companies, groups, or individuals. It has usually been for theft and fraud but it, too, can feed into surveillance and the misuse of information. Moreover, computerized systems like power grids and air traffic control systems are vulnerable to hacking that can disable essential infrastructure. Hacking is also basic to what has come to be called cyber warfare, mostly between states on the supranational level. Notable examples of such hacking by Russia, North Korea, the United States, and Israel have already taken place.[75] But the techniques of cyber warfare could obviously be turned by governments against their own citizens and might even serve a takeover and concentration of power within a given country or region.

Much of the discussion of the potentially negative implications of the new technologies involves hypothetical, worst-case scenarios, and the dangers can be overdramatized. But even if, for now at least, the object of concern lies partly in the realm of dystopian fantasy, the totalitarian category illuminates the dangers and helps us ponder the implications of present directions. Nightmarish scenarios are surely conceivable, and we need vigilance to preclude cyber totalitarianism from our future.

Adjusting the concept in light of new experience

We have seen that precisely because totalitarianism, appropriately recast, is best understood as only a direction, not a system, it need not be considered an either/or proposition. We have also seen that, brought to bear flexibly, the category helps us assess recent phenomena – even if they do not qualify as totalitarian overall. It helps considerably to see why this or that is not totalitarian. So the category illuminates both totalitarianism and the limit to its reach. As long as it remains reasonably adaptable and is applied flexibly, it is likely to remain in our arsenal to help us analyze future phenomena.

Yet even as some authorities are arguably too quick to invoke totalitarianism, others seem reluctant to use it even as a measuring rod, let alone as a full-blown characterization. At the same time, we find observers groping to characterize this or that novel phenomenon they usefully pinpoint – and usually lament. The reluctance to use the term "totalitarianism" is often paired with a preference for the authoritarianism category, but the preference seems unthinking, without consideration of why totalitarianism might be more illuminating, at least as a question to be raised.

Among the authorities we have encountered, Wenfang Tang is most explicit in recognizing the need to adjust categories in light of new experience, but he seems disinclined to use "totalitarianism." Treating contemporary China in his *Populist Authoritarianism*, he suggests that we have long tended to make the difference between democratic and certain undemocratic regimes too stark. Comparative political studies over the past half-century, made possible by large-scale comparative survey data, have undermined the long-standing association of "civic culture" with liberal democracy. In fact, Tang suggests, "liberal democracy may not be a very useful variable in explaining why people participate in politics, why they identify with their country, why the government responds to public demand, and why people trust their political system and each other." At issue is "social capital," which can be used to consolidate autocratic as well as democratic governments. By implication, we simply need a broader understanding of political participation and support, with less a priori privilege shown to democracy. For Tang, this means especially that the traditional understanding of authoritarianism, showing how political elites control the masses, needs to be refined to allow more room for regime support, political participation, and regime responsiveness.[76]

But Tang settles for a contrast between elite authoritarianism – demobilizing bureaucratic authoritarian states, like those of Latin America from the 1960s to the 1980s – and the populist authoritarianism of contemporary China.[77] Embracing, as he plausibly insists it does, popular participation in politics, trust in government, and government responsiveness, that populist authoritarianism does not conform to the totalitarian stereotype, but it has much in common with totalitarianism as appropriately recast. Tang's reluctance to use totalitarianism seems surprising partly because he endorses the earlier argument of Sheri Berman on the transition from Weimar democracy to the Nazi regime in Germany.[78] Challenging convention, she showed how civic culture and social capital did not help preserve democracy and resist Nazi totalitarianism but actually facilitated the transition to Nazi rule. Moreover, Berman's understanding of social capital suggests precisely the sort of reciprocity we found in earlier totalitarianism.

Tang does refer to totalitarianism, though he understands it in a somewhat stereotypical way even as he usefully seeks to split the difference in wrestling with the overall characterization. He notes, first, that some see the mass line as totalitarian, with the party manipulating the masses, whereas others see the mass line as empowering society, even providing a new mode of democratic decision making.[79] But, as Tang sees it, neither is correct, although it is the contrast with totalitarianism that matters for us: "Totalitarianism," he asserts, "focuses on the total control of the society by the state, while the Mass Line can be described as 'totalist politics' which is built on the full-scale interaction between the state and society."[80]

In fact, all three of the classical totalitarian regimes were closer to the mass line than to Tang's stereotypical notion of totalitarianism. Nonetheless, we wonder about the quality of the interaction and participation in those earlier regimes. We may assume that they were merely nominal, but we need more open-minded research to deepen our understanding. In the case of communist China, Tang and others have shown that the government seeks to be genuinely responsive, with both leaders and led taking the consultation system quite seriously.

In discussing the cyber threat, Alexander Klimburg similarly prefers authoritarianism, but he does not consider the possibility of adjustment as Tang does. Speaking of Putin's Russia, Klimburg notes almost casually that "as in all authoritarian states, regime stability is the overriding purpose of all aspects of the government."[81] That may be true up to a point for some earlier authoritarian states, but it seems misleading or incomplete with respect to Russia and the modern situation more generally. In a cyber world, given the scope for information, communication, and opposition, regime security may require something closer to totalitarianism than authoritarianism. It may require mobilization through disinformation, to convince people that, say, American machinations are behind every protest.

The examples of Tang and Klimburg suggest, most basically, the need to expand the totalitarianism category, especially beyond the earlier totalitarianism–authoritarianism binary. With an expanded palette, Klimburg would not so readily assume that authoritarianism provides an adequate explanation for Russian cyber behavior.

Relating to totalitarians and learning from experience

Assessing the future of the concept requires probing its ongoing utility for engaging the cases we have already experienced, both classic and subsequent, as we seek to understand them more deeply. I emphasized in chapter 1 that the concept came to have profoundly negative implications. And, for the most part, we remain concerned to prevent any recurrence of totalitarianism in the western mainstream and to limit or undercut it where we find it elsewhere.

However, that effort may require better learning through deeper engagement with those who have actually welcomed a radical, systematic alternative to western liberal democracy. And if such engagement is our aim, we might seem better off abandoning the totalitarianism category altogether in light of the negativity surrounding it. But even as we continue to take it as negative, we need not use totalitarianism as a term of abuse, denigration, or condescension, warranting only a delimited mode of engagement. To characterize the anti-liberal alternative as totalitarian is not in itself to excoriate it, to impute evil, or to preclude conversation.

However, we must address two modes of engagement – triumphalism and universalism – that prove the under-lying obstacles to a mode of engagement that might serve deeper understanding. Up to a point, these obstacles are disparate, insofar as triumphalism has negative connotations and universalism may seem noble. But we quickly discern a comparable arrogance that makes each an obstacle to under-standing. In a sense, they are two sides of the same coin.

Even as communism continued in the Soviet bloc, the fate of the Mussolini, Hitler, and Stalin departures bred confidence in the superiority of liberal democracy and a concomitant assumption that totalitarianism could never recur within the western mainstream. But this attitude displayed a certain triumphalist complacency that arguably kept us from learning all we could from the historical experience. Indeed, that triumphalism fed the stereotypical version of totalitarianism, with the concomitant pitfalls of essentialism, reductionism, and teleology that sometimes made it more an impediment than an aid to understanding.

But this triumphalist complacency has prompted periodic warnings that whereas we do indeed need to engage totalitar-ianism to prevent recurrence and to shore up our democracy, we are not doing it very well. Fleeing Nazi Germany first for London, then for America, Sigmund Neumann usefully insisted that the democratic self-understanding, and even its associated vocabulary, required renewal in light of the totalitarian challenge: "This is of primary importance for the survival of democracy, which, of all forms of society, is most dependent on 'mutual understanding.'" And such renewal required serious engagement with the totalitarian challenge on the conceptual level.[82] Such subsequent works as Stephen Holmes's *The Anatomy of Antiliberalism* (1993) and Michael

Halberstam's *Totalitarianism and the Modern Conception of Politics* (1999) similarly addressed what had been learned, and what could have been better learned, from engaging with the earlier totalitarian experience.[83] Each implied that a tendency toward liberal triumphalism had kept us from learning all that we might.

Deeper encounter with the totalitarian experiments enables us better to understand what we believe instead and why. Pluralism, individualism, and freedom are surely central but, especially in light of the negative outcomes of the earlier totalitarianism, these ideals can become facile, invoked almost ritualistically. We may proclaim "the rule of law," for example, but as we have noted "the rule of law" is not decisive as an antidote to totalitarianism. We recall Alfredo Rocco and the only semi-tongue-in-cheek characterization featured by Karl Deutsch that "under totalitarianism, everything that is not forbidden is compulsory." Sharia, too, could entail the rule of law and still be totalitarian. And whatever our doubts about J. L. Talmon's way of tracing the totalitarian impulse back to the era of the French Revolution, his insistence that democracy can be totalitarian remains valuable; democracy is no guarantee against totalitarian excess. There are various modes of democracy, however, and specifying *liberal* democracy is better. But just how real, in actual practice, are the rights, freedoms, and democratic procedures we trumpet?

In any case, by the early twenty-first century, triumphalist complacency was diminishing as even western liberal democracy came to seem less secure, and as anti-liberal forces were clearly alive, and perhaps even ascendant, in much of the world. So resistance certainly remains an imperative, but insofar as we become less complacent, we come to understand the challenge and the possibilities for confronting it a bit differently. But do we adopt a more open approach to past and present instances, much as we continue to dislike them? Or are we more likely to get our backs up and make more explicit the claim to universality implicitly underlying the earlier triumphalism?

According to well-meaning critics of Islamic extremism like Bassam Tibi, Muslims need to recognize that the cultural and legal underpinnings of democracy are not western impositions but universal, based on the primacy of reason, and accessible to all cultures. Conversely, totalitarianism is anti-modern and part of the anti-rational counter-Enlightenment.[84] We are quick to claim universality based on reason, as if reason specifies democracy and human rights, as if rationalism, democracy, and human rights all come together neatly. But the relationships are more problematic in both theory and practice. To be sure, Tibi claims not that these values are universally held, only that they are accessible to all. But that only helps so much. Radical Islamism, too, is accessible to all.

In arguing for universality, Tibi observed that the notion of "westernization," once fundamental, has been utterly discredited in academic circles. Indeed, he went on, some US scholars go to the opposite extreme and, adopting a mode of cultural relativism, depict Islamism as a legitimate mode of opposition to westernization, an alternative model of development, a plausible response to the crisis of modernity.[85] Tibi does not buy the argument, and neither does the present author. The key is the scope for dissenting on a basis different from Tibi's problematic universalism.

The alternative does not have to mean settling for cultural relativism, though we must keep in mind one of Michael Halberstam's key points. He suggested that rather than face up to the fact that the liberal political community, like the totalitarian, is dependent on a "nonrational historically shared common sense which is not neutral with regard to competing conceptions of the good," liberals tend simply to invoke the threat of totalitarianism to justify liberalism.[86] With this formulation, Halberstam surely offers no basis for a liberal claim to universality or privilege. Indeed, what he pinpoints is more like circularity: we feel superior simply because we are not totalitarian.

We may still reject Islamic extremism and totalitarianism in general on the basis of dominant western values. But as of now they have not been made universal, and it can seem mere arbitrary wishful thinking to claim that they are. However, we may seek to spread our values – even to make them universal – through engagement and persuasion. There is obviously limited scope for engagement with Islamic extremists who claim that sacred texts provide all the answers. At issue is not the scope for converting ISIS or the Taliban but conversation with those uncertain or conflicted. As it is, however, our arguments can too often be shown up as self-serving and hypocritical. We recall Brian Taylor's reference to the combustible relationship between the defensive, hypersensitive Vladimir Putin and "American tendencies toward sanctimoniousness about the universality of its liberal and democratic values and its perceived benign role in the world."

Some find totalitarian implications even in our claim of universal reason. Alexander Dugin's assertion to that effect, noted above, seems self-serving and overstated, but the same point is implicit in Tzetvan Todorov's warning that any movement toward a world state, even a "drift toward unification" based on the notion that one size fits all, is dangerous and indeed totalitarian in implication. The alternative – the antidote – is pluralism, checks and balances, a balance of power. At the same time Todorov cautioned that the West needs to avoid excessive intervention and overreach stemming from a claim of universal responsibility to cure all ills. For example, it was probably better that the West did not intervene to stop atrocities in Cambodia or Rwanda, leaving it to the neighboring countries – Vietnam and Uganda, respectively.[87]

Todorov's concerns are certainly plausible, but we need not reject altogether the universalist aspiration, which in principle can be compatible with the pluralism he features. We have come to agree across cultures, recognizing certain human rights, and in that sense they have become universal. After all, avoiding a totalizing universalism as we seek to persuade does not mean that, in the name of pluralism, we must countenance cannibalism, human sacrifice, or slavery after all. And there is surely scope for further agreement. If we do come to agree, so much the better, but insofar as we do not, operating as if we in the West were uniquely universal is counterproductive.

What contemporary Russia, China, and radical Islam have in common is a claim to offer an alternative to the hegemonic West, hypocritically, as they see it, claiming universality. That contemporary anti-liberal argument is comparable to the earlier totalitarian claim to be leapfrogging mainstream liberal modernity. We surely must fight back but doing so effectively requires deeper learning through closer engagement with those who have not found the western liberal model universal and who, in fact, particularly dislike our assertions of universality. As we continue the contest, totalitarianism remains central to what must be understood.

Notes

Chapter 1 Why Should We Care about Totalitarianism?

1 Tzvetan Todorov, *Hope and Memory* (London: Atlantic, 2003), 2.
2 Karl W. Deutsch, "Cracks in the Monolith: Possibilities and Patterns of Disintegration in Totalitarian Systems," in Carl J. Friedrich (ed.), *Totalitarianism* (Cambridge: Harvard University Press, 1954), 309.
3 Mao Zedong's name was rendered in English as Mao Tse-tung before the reform of the transliteration of the Chinese language in 1982, so he is referred to by that name in older works.
4 *Evelyn Cameron: Pictures from a Worthy Life* (Montana PBS; Missoula: University of Montana, 2005).
5 Anna Burns, *Milkman: A Novel* (Minneapolis: Graywolf Press, 2018), 25, 120, 172.
6 Masha Gessen, *The Future is History: How Totalitarianism Reclaimed Russia* (New York: Riverhead, 2017).
7 Michael Geyer and Sheila Fitzpatrick (eds), *Beyond Totalitarianism: Stalinism and Nazism Compared* (Cambridge: Cambridge University Press, 2009).
8 Michael David-Fox, Introduction to Michael David-Fox, Peter Holquist, and Alexander M. Martin (eds), *Fascination and Enmity: Russia and Germany as Entangled Histories, 1914–1945* (Pittsburgh: University of Pittsburgh Press, 2012), 3.

9   Richard Overy, *The Dictators: Hitler's Germany and Stalin's Russia* (New York: Norton, 2004), xxvii, 73.
10   Irving Howe, *Politics and the Novel* (New York: Meridian, 1987 [1967]), 249–50.

Chapter 2 The Career of a Concept

1   Abbott Gleason, *Totalitarianism: The Inner History of the Cold War* (New York: Oxford University Press, 1995), 19.
2   Ibid., 9, 19, 94–5.
3   The key statement of Gentile's fascism is his *Origini e dottrina del fascismo* (1929); see the exemplary translation by A. James Gregor, *Origins and Doctrine of Fascism, with Selections from Other Works* (New Brunswick: Transaction, 2002).
4   Carl Schmitt, *State, Movement, People* (Corvallis: Plutarch, 2001).
5   Franz Neumann, *Behemoth: The Structure and Practice of National Socialism, 1933–1944* (New York: Harper Torchbooks, 1966 [1944]; from 2nd edn), 64–5.
6   Aristotle Kallis, "Neither Fascist nor Authoritarian: The 4th of August Regime in Greece (1936–1941) and the Dynamics of Fascistisation in 1930s Europe," *East Central Europe* 37 (2010): 307, 313.
7   Peter F. Drucker, *The End of Economic Man: The Origins of Totalitarianism* (New York: Harper Colophon, 1969 [1939]), 244–7.
8   Ibid., 129.
9   Ibid., 133–4, 139–40.
10   Ibid., 219–23, 227–31, 234.
11   James Burnham, *The Managerial Revolution: What is Happening in the World* (New York: John Day, 1941), 160–1, 167–71.
12   Ibid., 152.
13   Karl R. Popper, *The Open Society and Its Enemies*, 1: *The Spell of Plato*, 5th edn (London: Routledge, 1966 [1945]), 1.
14   Karl R. Popper, *The Open Society and Its Enemies*, 2: *The High Tide of Prophecy: Hegel, Marx, and the Aftermath*, 5th edn (London: Routledge, 1966 [1945]).
15   Popper, *The Open Society*, 1: 17. See also Karl R. Popper, *The Poverty of Historicism* (New York: Harper & Row [Harper Torchbooks], 1964 [1957]).
16   Popper, *The Open Society*, 1:1.

17 Carl J. Friedrich and Zbigniew Brzezinski, *Totalitarian Dictatorship and Autocracy*, 2nd edn (New York: Praeger, 1965 [1956]), 16–17, 408 n. 284.

18 J. L. Talmon, *The Origins of Totalitarian Democracy* (New York: Norton, 1970; first published 1952), 1, 249.

19 Ibid., 6–7.

20 Ibid., 2, 9, 254.

21 Ibid., 1–3, 5.

22 Ibid., 254–5.

23 Norman Cohn, *The Pursuit of the Millennium: Revolutionary Messianism in Medieval and Reformation Europe and Its Bearing on Modern Totalitarian Movements*, 2nd edn (New York: Harper Torchbooks, 1961 [1957]), vi–vii.

24 Ibid., 318–19.

25 Ibid., 122, 308–12.

26 Ibid., 319.

27 Ibid., 313–15.

28 Richard Shorten, *Modernism and Totalitarianism: Rethinking the Intellectual Sources of Nazism and Stalinism, 1945 to the Present* (Houndmills: Palgrave Macmillan, 2012), 70.

29 Talmon, *The Origins of Totalitarian Democracy*, 9.

30 George Orwell, "James Burnham and the Managerial Revolution" (1946), in George Orwell, *The Collected Essays, Journalism and Letters*, 4: *In Front of Your Nose, 1946–1950* (Boston: David R. Godine, 2000), 170–3, 178–89.

31 George Orwell, *Nineteen Eighty-Four* (New York: Harcourt Brace, 1983), 221–2.

32 George Orwell, "The Prevention of Literature," in Orwell, *Collected Essays*, 4: 63–4.

33 Thomas Pynchon, Foreword to Orwell, *Nineteen Eighty-Four*, xxii–xxiii; Orwell, *Nineteen Eighty-Four*, 170–1.

34 Orwell, *Nineteen Eighty-Four*, 257–8, 265–7, 300, 308.

35 Ibid., 195, 203–4, 270–2.

36 Irving Howe, *Politics and the Novel* (New York: Meridian, 1987 [1967]), 250.

37 Hannah Arendt, *The Origins of Totalitarianism* (Cleveland: Meridian, 1958). The added portion, "Ideology and Terror: A Novel Form of Government," was originally a 1950 lecture so it is from essentially the same period as the original book.

38 Peter Baehr, *Hannah Arendt, Totalitarianism, and the Social Sciences* (Stanford: Stanford University Press, 2010), 19, 82, 102, 139.

39 Arendt, *The Origins of Totalitarianism*, 447.

40 Ibid., 458, 462–6, 470.
41 Ibid., 318.
42 Ibid., 458; see also 407, 417–18.
43 Ibid., 437–8, 457, 463–6.
44 Ibid., 462–6; see also 325–6, 391–2, 398–9.
45 Baehr, *Hannah Arendt*, 88.
46 David Riesman, *Individualism Reconsidered and Other Essays* (1954), 409–25. See especially Baehr, *Hannah Arendt*, 45–50, on the correspondence between Riesman and Arendt.
47 Raymond Aron, *In Defense of Political Reason* (Lanham: Rowman & Littlefield, 1994), 98.
48 Baehr, *Hannah Arendt*, 51–2, 55–6.
49 Friedrich and Brzezinski, *Totalitarian Dictatorship*, vii–viii, xi, 14, 18–19.
50 Ibid., 19–21.
51 Ibid., 3–4, 15, 27.
52 Ibid., 16.
53 Ibid., 15, 17,
54 Ibid., 21–2.
55 Ibid., 8.
56 Ibid., 277–339.
57 Ibid., 17–18.
58 Ibid., 9.
59 Ibid., 26.
60 Ibid., 25–6.
61 Robert Jay Lifton, *Thought Reform and the Psychology of Totalism: A Study of "Brainwashing" in China* (New York: Norton, 1963), 248.
62 Ibid., 5.
63 Ibid., 4–5.
64 Ibid., 245.
65 Ibid., 13.
66 Ibid., 420.
67 Ibid., 429.
68 Herbert Marcuse, *One-Dimensional Man: Studies in the Ideology of Advanced Industrial Society* (Boston: Beacon, 1964), 3.
69 Ibid., xv.
70 Ibid., 12.
71 Ibid., 171–9.
72 Ibid., xv–xvi, 14.
73 See, for example, Simon Susen, *The "Postmodern Turn" in the Social Sciences* (Basingstoke: Palgrave Macmillan, 2015).
74 Czesław Miłosz, *The Captive Mind* (New York: Knopf, 1953).

75 Milovan Djilas, *The New Class: An Analysis of the Communist System* (New York: Praeger, 1957).

76 Shorten, *Modernism and Totalitarianism*, 56.

77 Timothy Garton Ash, *The Magic Lantern: The Revolution of '89 Witnessed in Warsaw, Budapest, Berlin and Prague* (New York: Vintage, 1993), 137.

78 Václav Havel et al., *The Power of the Powerless: Citizens Against the State in Central Eastern Europe* (Armonk: Sharpe, 1985), 27–31, 36–7.

79 Stéphane Courtois, Nicolas Werth et al. (eds), *The Black Book of Communism: Crimes, Terror, Repression* (Cambridge: Harvard University Press, 1999).

80 Enzo Traverso, *Il totalitarismo: Storia di un dibattito*. Milan: Bruno Mondadori, 2002; Anson Rabinbach, "Moments of Totalitarianism," *History and Theory*, 45, no. 1 (Feb. 2006): 72–100.

81 Primo Levi, *Survival in Auschwitz: The Nazi Assault on Humanity* (New York: Simon & Schuster [Touchstone], 1996). The book was initially published under a different title and has an extremely complex publication history.

82 See, for example, Langer's introduction to Lawrence Langer (ed.), *Art from the Ashes: A Holocaust Anthology* (New York: Oxford University Press, 1995), 5.

83 Tim Cole, *Selling the Holocaust: From Auschwitz to Schindler: How History Is Bought, Packaged, and Sold* (New York: Routledge, 1999), 4. The book was published in the United Kingdom by Duckworth as *Images of the Holocaust*.

84 For example, Giorgio Agamben, *Remnants of Auschwitz* (New York: Zone, 1999).

85 Christopher Dillon, *Dachau and the SS: A Schooling in Violence* (Oxford: Oxford University Press, 2015).

86 Tzvetan Todorov, *Facing the Extreme: Moral Life in the Concentration Camps* (New York: Henry Holt, 1996 [original French edition 1991]).

87 Tzvetan Todorov, *Hope and Memory* (London: Atlantic, 2003 [2000]), 301.

88 Ibid., 78–9, 124, 209–10.

89 Ibid., 159–64.

90 Slavoj Žižek, *Did Somebody Say Totalitarianism? Five Interventions on the (Mis)use of a Notion* (London: Verso, 2001), 3.

91 Ibid., 127–8.

92 Ibid., 131–2.

93 Ibid., 229, 256.

94 Ibid., 6.
95 Ibid., 141.
96 Ibid., 66–8.
97 Roger Griffin, *A Fascist Century* (Houndmills: Palgrave Macmillan, 2008), 63.
98 Emilio Gentile, *Le religioni della politica: Fra democrazie e totalitarismi* (Rome and Bari: Laterza, 2001), xvii–xviii.
99 Emilio Gentile, "Fascism, Totalitarianism and Political Religion: Definitions and Critical Reflections on Criticisms of an Interpretation," in Roger Griffin (ed.), *Fascism, Totalitarianism and Political Religion* (London: Routledge, 2005), 65–6.
100 Todorov, *Hope and Memory*, 29, 113–16.
101 Ibid., 26–7.
102 Ibid., 18–20, 283.
103 Ibid., 33–4, 141–2.
104 Ibid., 32–3.
105 Ibid., 40.
106 Ibid., 19–26.
107 Ibid., 25–6.
108 David D. Roberts, *The Totalitarian Experiment in Twentieth-Century Europe: Understanding the Poverty of Great Politics* (London: Routledge, 2006).
109 Shorten, *Modernism and Totalitarianism*, 248, n. 20.
110 Ibid., 24.
111 Ibid., 50, 240–1.
112 Ibid., 4.
113 Ibid., 132.
114 Ibid., 167; see also 165–6.
115 Ibid., 170.
116 Ibid., 175–6.
117 Ibid., 60.
118 Ibid., 40–2, 240.

Chapter 3 Totalitarian Trajectories During the Era of the Two World Wars

1 Richard Overy, *The Dictators: Hitler's Germany and Stalin's Russia* (New York: Norton, 2004), xxvii, 73; see also 73–5, 636–7, where openings for recasting are let drop.
2 Michael Geyer and Sheila Fitzpatrick (eds), *Beyond Totalitarianism: Stalinism and Nazism Compared* (Cambridge: Cambridge University Press, 2009).

3   Emilio Gentile, *La via italiana al totalitarismo: Il partito e lo Stato nel regime fascista* (Rome: La Nuova Italia Scientifica, 1995), 148–53.

4   Camillo Pellizzi, *Problemi e realtà del fascismo* (Florence: Vallecchi, 1924), 157–65.

5   David D. Roberts, *The Syndicalist Tradition and Italian Fascism* (Chapel Hill: University of North Carolina Press, 1979), chs 6, 7, and 10.

6   Giuseppe Bottai, *Esperienza corporativa (1929–1934)* (Florence: Vallecchi, 1934), 584–94.

7   Benito Mussolini, *Scritti e discorsi di Benito Mussolini*, 6 (Milan: Ulrico Hoepli, 1934), 77.

8   Ibid., 5: 162.

9   Detlev J. K. Peukert, *The Weimar Republic: The Crisis of Classical Modernity* (New York: Hill and Wang, 1993), 134–6, 271–2.

10 Ian Kershaw, *Hitler, 1889–1936: Hubris* (New York: Norton, 1998), 93, 132, 311, 314, 437, 529–32.

11 Peter Fritzsche, *Life and Death in the Third Reich* (Cambridge: Harvard University Press, 2008); Thomas Kühne, *Belonging and Genocide: Hitler's Community, 1918–1945* (New Haven: Yale University Press, 2010).

12 Eric A. Johnson, *Nazi Terror: The Gestapo, Jews, and Ordinary Germans* (New York: Basic Books, 1999); Robert Gellately, *Backing Hitler: Consent and Coercion in Nazi Germany* (Oxford: Oxford University Press, 2001).

13 See, for example, Michael Wildt, *Hitler's* Volksgemeinschaft *and the Dynamics of Racial Exclusion: Violence Against Jews in Provincial Germany, 1919–1939* (New York: Berghahn, 2012).

14 Cited in Karl Dietrich Bracher, *The Nazi Dictatorship: The Origins, Structure, and Effects of National Socialism* (New York: Praeger, 1970), 340.

15 Michael Burleigh, *Death and Deliverance: "Euthanasia" in Germany, c. 1900–1945* (Cambridge: Cambridge University Press, 1994), 4.

16 Karl A. Schleunes, *The Twisted Road to Auschwitz: Nazi Policy Toward German Jews, 1933–1939* (Urbana: University of Illinois Press, 1990).

17 Christopher R. Browning, *The Path to Genocide: Essays on Launching the Final Solution* (Cambridge: Cambridge University Press, 1992), 7.

18 Saul Friedlander, *Memory, History, and the Extermination of*

the Jews of Europe (Bloomington: Indiana University Press, 1993), 109–11.

Chapter 4 Movements and Regimes Since World War II

1 Timothy Cheek, "Mao, Revolution, and Memory," in Timothy Cheek (ed.), *A Critical Introduction to Mao* (Cambridge: Cambridge University Press, 2010), 13.
2 Robert Jay Lifton, *Thought Reform and the Psychology of Totalism: A Study of "Brainwashing" in China* (New York: Norton, 1963), 260, 394–5.
3 Ibid., 262, 270; Cheek, "Mao, Revolution, and Memory," 14.
4 Lifton, *Thought Reform*, 412–13.
5 Cheek, "Mao, Revolution, and Memory," 14; Hans J. Van de Ven, "War, Cosmopolitanism, and Authority: Mao from 1937 to 1956," in Cheek (ed.), *A Critical Introduction to Mao*, 96; Wenfang Tang, *Populist Authoritarianism: Chinese Political Culture and Regime Sustainability* (New York: Oxford University Press, 2016), 5–6, 8–9.
6 Jiang Yihua and Roderick MacFarquhar, "Two Perspectives on Mao Zedong," in Cheek (ed.), *A Critical Introduction to Mao*, 348.
7 Teresa Wright, *Party and State in Post-Mao China* (Cambridge: Polity Press, 2015), 153.
8 Cheek, "Mao, Revolution, and Memory," 12.
9 Susan L. Shirk, "The Decline of Virtuocracy in China," in James L. Watson (ed.), *Class and Social Stratification in Post-Revolution China* (Cambridge: Cambridge University Press, 1984), 57.
10 Ibid., 69, 71.
11 Ibid., 62–3, 71.
12 Ibid., 58, 61, 67, 70, 73, 78.
13 Cheek, "Mao, Revolution, and Memory," 13.
14 Wright, *Party and State in Post-Mao China*, 1.
15 Ibid., 3–4, 181–2.
16 Tang, *Populist Authoritarianism*, 8.
17 Ibid., 57.
18 Cheek, "Mao, Revolution, and Memory," 18–19.
19 Albert J. Bergesen (ed.), *The Sayyid Qutb Reader: Selected Writings on Politics, Religion, and Society* (New York: Routledge, 2008), 11–12.

20 For example, Mehdi Mozaffari, *Islamism: A New Totalitarianism* (Boulder: Lynne Rienner, 2017), 276; Hamed Abdel-Samad, *Islamic Fascism* (New York: Prometheus, 2016), 34; Bassam Tibi, *Islamism and Islam* (New Haven: Yale University Press, 2012), 1, 4, 15–16, 25–6, 39.

21 Mozaffari, *Islamism*, 22, 110–11, 246, 267.

22 Tzvetan Todorov, *Hope and Memory* (London: Atlantic, 2003), xiv.

23 Peter Baehr, *Hannah Arendt, Totalitarianism, and the Social Sciences* (Stanford: Stanford University Press, 2010), 139–44.

24 Tibi, *Islamism and Islam*, 1, 4, 15–16, 25–6, 39.

25 Abdel-Samad, *Islamic Fascism*, 22; see also 46, 52–3, 188–9.

26 Mozaffari, *Islamism*, 284.

27 Tibi, *Islamism and Islam*, 47–8.

28 Abdel-Samad, *Islamic Fascism*, 28–9, 32.

29 Bergesen (ed.), *The Sayyid Qutb Reader*, 16–19, 21.

30 Tibi, *Islamism and Islam*, 15–16, 39, 44.

31 Bergesen (ed.), *The Sayyid Qutb Reader*, 9–10.

32 William O. Beeman, "Post-Revolutionary Iran: Democracy or Theocracy?," in Mahmood Monshipouri (ed.), *Inside the Islamic Republic: Social Change in Post-Khomeini Iran* (Oxford: Oxford University Press, 2016), 59–61.

33 Tibi, *Islamism and Islam*, 168–9.

34 Ibid., 4, 24–5, 39, 110, 160–1, 164, 167, 172.

35 Bergesen (ed.), *The Sayyid Qutb Reader*, 12; Mozaffari, *Islamism*, 44–6; Abdel-Samad, *Islamic Fascism*, 56, 58, 63.

36 Tibi, *Islamism and Islam*, 140–1.

37 Ibid., 49–50, 135, 138, 161.

38 Mozaffari, *Islamism*, 149, 164–5.

39 Tibi, *Islamism and Islam*, 23, 134, 219.

40 Ibid., 23, 135.

41 Ibid., 16–17; Mozaffari, *Islamism*, 272–3.

42 Mozaffari, *Islamism*, 87.

43 Ibid., 257, 274.

44 Tibi, *Islamism and Islam*, 27.

45 Abdel-Samad, *Islamic Fascism*, 120.

46 Michael Axworthy, *Revolutionary Iran: A History of the Islamic Republic* (Oxford: Oxford University Press, 2013), 415.

47 Anoushiravan Ehteshami, *Iran: Stuck in Transition* (London: Routledge, 2017), 25.

48 Axworthy, *Revolutionary Iran*, 139.

49 Beeman, "Post-Revolutionary Iran," 48.

50 Axworthy, *Revolutionary Iran*, 96, 319–20.

51 Beeman, "Post-Revolutionary Iran," 60.
52 Axworthy, *Revolutionary Iran*, 414.
53 Ehteshami, *Iran*, 269.
54 Mozaffari, *Islamism*, 95–6.
55 Axworthy, *Revolutionary Iran*, 147–8; Beeman, "Post-Revolutionary Iran," 53.
56 Ehteshami, *Iran*, 5, 7.
57 Quoted in Axworthy, *Revolutionary Iran*, 245.
58 Ibid., 224.
59 Ibid., 413.
60 Ehteshami, *Iran*, 250, 256–7.
61 Ibid., 253–5, 271.
62 Ibid., 268, 274.
63 Ibid., 274.
64 Axworthy, *Revolutionary Iran*, 352, 418.
65 Ehteshami, *Iran*, 39.
66 Ibid., 9–10; Axworthy, *Revolutionary Iran*, 242, 313.
67 Beeman, "Post-Revolutionary Iran," 60.
68 Axworthy, *Revolutionary Iran*, 152–3.
69 Ehteshami, *Iran*, 11.
70 Ibid., 43; Axworthy, *Revolutionary Iran*, 313.
71 Axworthy, *Revolutionary Iran*, 208–9.
72 Ibid., 413–14.
73 Ibid., 415.
74 Ehteshami, *Iran*, 273.
75 Axworthy, *Revolutionary Iran*, 410–11.
76 Beeman, "Post-Revolutionary Iran," 48–9.

Chapter 5 The Future of Totalitarianism

1 Roger Griffin, "Uniqueness and Family Resemblances in Generic Fascism," *East Central Europe* 37 (2010): 339.
2 Slavoj Žižek, *Did Somebody Say Totalitarianism? Five Interventions on the (Mis)use of a Notion* (London: Verso, 2001), 22.
3 Roger Griffin, *Fascism: An Introduction to Comparative Fascist Studies* (Cambridge: Polity, 2018).
4 Brian D. Taylor, *The Code of Putinism* (New York: Oxford University Press, 2018), 4, 44.
5 Ibid., 18.
6 Alexander Klimburg, *The Darkening Web: The War for Cyberspace* (New York: Penguin Press, 2017), 212–13.

7   Ibid., 105–6, 324–5.
8   Gerard Toal, *Near Abroad: Putin, the West, and the Contest over Ukraine and the Caucasus* (New York: Oxford University Press, 2017), 205.
9   Ibid., 76–9, 205.
10   Alexander Dugin, *The Fourth Political Theory* (London: Arktos, 2018), 46, 52–3, 57–8, 61.
11   Ibid., 53–6, 67. The quotation is from 56.
12   Ibid., 46.
13   Robert Cottrell, "Russia's Gay Demons," *New York Review of Books,* December 7, 2017, 36, 38.
14   Taylor, *The Code of Putinism*, 29.
15   Cottrell, "Russia's Gay Demons," 38.
16   Ibid., 37.
17   Ibid.
18   Mikhail Zygar, *All the Kremlin's Men: Inside the Court of Vladimir Putin* (New York: Public Affairs, 2016), xx.
19   Taylor, *The Code of Putinism*, 35, 41.
20   Ibid., 177–9; the quoted passage is from 179.
21   Ibid., 53–4.
22   Ibid., 106–7, 118–20.
23   Ibid., 4–5, 44, 122, 204; the quoted passage is from 198.
24   Ibid., 2, 11, 23.
25   Toal, *Near Abroad*, 26, 32–3.
26   Ibid., 20.
27   Taylor, *The Code of Putinism*, 166–73, 192.
28   "A New Form of Totalitarianism Takes Root in China," *The Washington Post*, February 26, 2018.
29   Elizabeth C. Economy, *The Third Revolution: Xi Jinping and the New Chinese State* (New York: Oxford University Press, 2018), 3, 8–10, 14.
30   Ibid., 30–1, 34–5; Wenfang Tang, *Populist Authoritarianism: Chinese Political Culture and Regime Sustainability* (New York: Oxford University Press, 2016), 153, 157.
31   Economy, *The Third Revolution*, 38–42.
32   Jacques deLisle, Avery Goldstein, and Guobin Yang, "Introduction," *The Internet, Social Media, and a Changing China* (Philadelphia: University of Pennsylvania Press, 2016), 1–3.
33   Klimburg, *The Darkening Web*, 259–60, 267–8, 273; Economy, *The Third Revolution*, 57, 76–8, 81, 83.
34   Jacob Weisberg, "The Autocracy App," *The New York Review of Books*, October 25, 2018, 22; David Owen, "Here's Looking at You," *The New Yorker*, December 17, 2018, 28–33.

35 Economy, *The Third Revolution*, 80.
36 Klimburg, *The Darkening Web*, 266–7.
37 Economy, *The Third Revolution*, 103–6, 108–10, 118.
38 Ibid., 161–3, 166–7, 171–2, 176–7, 184.
39 James Millward, "'Reeducating' Xinjiang's Muslims," *New York Review of Books*, February 7, 2019, 38.
40 Ibid., 39.
41 Ibid., 38, 41.
42 Ibid., 39–40.
43 Tang, *Populist Authoritarianism*, 155.
44 DeLisle, Goldstein, and Yang, "Introduction," 4, 20–1, 24; Wright, *Party and State in Post-Mao China*, 93.
45 Economy, *The Third Revolution*, 119, 122–3, 132.
46 Ibid., 190–6.
47 Ibid., 59, 141, 150, 218–21.
48 Tang, *Populist Authoritarianism*, 1.
49 DeLisle, Goldstein, and Yang, "Introduction," 26.
50 Ibid., 3.
51 Wright, *Party and State in Post-Mao China*, 12–13, 58, 142, 144.
52 Tang, *Populist Authoritarianism*, 1–2, 156–7.
53 Ahmed S. Hashim, *The Caliphate at War: Operational Realities and Innovations of the Islamic State* (New York: Oxford University Press, 2018), 60–1.
54 Joby Warrick, *Black Flags: The Rise of Isis* (New York: Anchor, 2016), 29, 170.
55 Hashim, *The Caliphate at War*, 8.
56 Ibid., 12.
57 Ibid., 254–60 (259 for the passage quoted); Warrick, *Black Flags*, 286–9.
58 Hashim, *The Caliphate at War*, 239–40; Warrick, *Black Flags*, 252.
59 Warrick, *Black Flags*, 172–4.
60 Ibid., 306–7, 311–14.
61 Hashim, *The Caliphate at War*, 5, 14, 241, 267, 269, 287, 293–4.
62 Ibid., 323.
63 Ben Taub, "Shallow Graves," *The New Yorker*, December 24 and 31, 2018.
64 Martin Malia, *The Soviet Tragedy: A History of Socialism in Russia, 1917–1991* (New York: Free Press, 1994), 516–20.
65 Žižek, *Did Somebody Say Totalitarianism?* 229–30, 256.
66 Tzvetan Todorov, *Hope and Memory* (London: Atlantic, 2003), 30–1.

67 Klimburg, *The Darkening Web*, 208–9.
68 Ibid., 185–91.
69 Ibid., 188.
70 Tamsin Shaw, "Beware the Big Five," *New York Review of Books*, April 5, 2018, 34.
71 Ibid., 35.
72 Ibid., 33.
73 Siva Vaidhyanathan, *Anti-Social Media: How Facebook Disconnects Us and Undermines Democracy* (New York: Oxford University Press, 2018).
74 Ibid., 2–3.
75 Klimburg, *The Darkening Web*, 59, 205–7, 180–1.
76 Tang, *Populist Authoritarianism*, 165–6. The quoted passage is from 165.
77 Ibid., 162–3, 166.
78 Ibid., 154–5; Sheri Berman, "Civil Society and the Collapse of the Weimar Republic," *World Politics* 49(3) (April 1997): 401–29.
79 Tang, *Populist Authoritarianism*, 7.
80 Ibid., 8.
81 Klimburg, *The Darkening Web*, 227.
82 Sigmund Neumann, *Permanent Revolution: The Total State in a World at War* (New York: Harper & Brothers, 1942), vii, x, xiv, 306–10.
83 Stephen Holmes, *The Anatomy of Antiliberalism* (Cambridge, Harvard University Press, 1993), 154; Michael Halberstam, *Totalitarianism and the Modern Conception of Politics* (New Haven: Yale University Press, 1999), 128, 133.
84 Bassam Tibi, *Islamism and Islam* (New Haven: Yale University Press, 2012), 116, 186, 237.
85 Ibid., 176.
86 Halberstam, *Totalitarianism and the Modern Conception of Politics*, 128, 133.
87 Todorov, *Hope and Memory*, 285–8.

Index